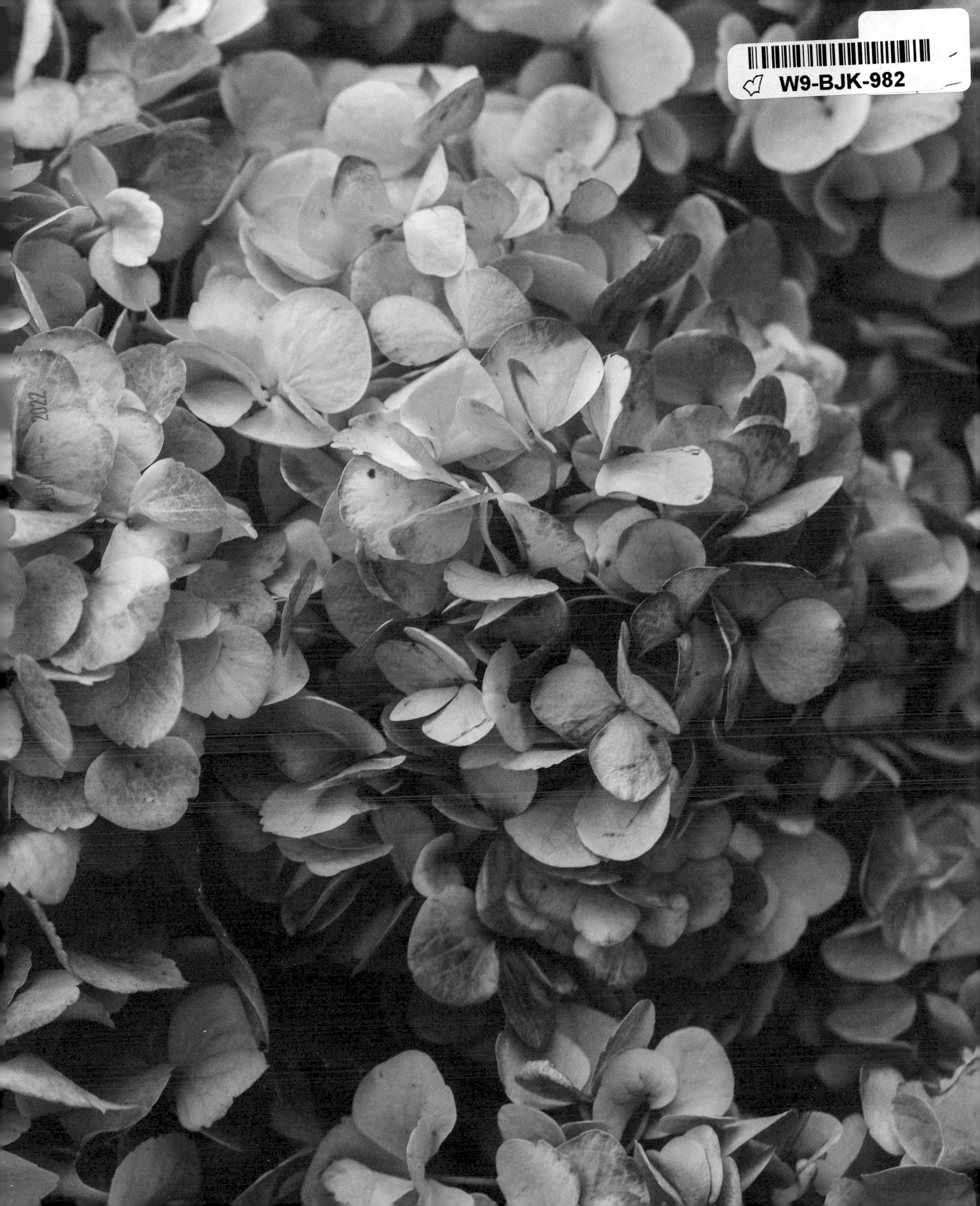

You're Invited

RIZZOLI
NEW YORK

New York · Paris · London · Milan

You're Invited

CLASSIC, ELEGANT ENTERTAINING

STEPHANIE BOOTH SHAFRAN

Written with Kathryn O'Shea-Evans
Foreword by Jeffrey Bilhuber
Photographed by Andrew and Gemma Ingalls

To my large, crazy family . . . natural and blended.

FOREWORD

Great entertaining is about great communication. My longtime friend and client Stephanie Booth Shafran is impressively articulate—effervescent and energetic. She deeply believes in the beauty that surrounds her, and knows how to share it with family and friends. All of the residences that I've created for Stephanie and her family are comfortable and inviting because they directly reflect who she is.

I think that's why Stephanie is such a great messenger for the entertaining lifestyle. The events she creates are true to her vision, but never appear labored or burdensome. Stephanie is a superb hostess: her parties are young, bright, fresh, and modern in their approach, while still firmly rooted in glorious tradition.

Stephanie is the product of a family that understands how powerfully important it is to be surrounded by people you admire and enjoy. She grew up witnessing firsthand that there is as much delight to be had in planning a party, as there is to be had in the party itself. She also understands that when working with the best, you're guaranteed the best results.

It's one thing to say, "I'd like to have a dinner party!" It's another to determine which drink to serve with the hors d'oeuvre, the best wines to pair with dinner, not to mention choosing place settings, flowers, and food that reinforce the concept and goals. Stephanie does this and more with imagination and confidence. She is as good a teacher as she is a hostess. In this book, Stephanie pulls back the curtain and lets us watch her in action. She generously shares great tips and knowledge gained from experience, and invites us to take in the memorable results. Let the entertaining begin!

—*Jeffrey Bilhuber*

INTRODUCTION

Being welcomed into someone's home for a soirée is one of life's greatest pleasures—whether the event is large or small, simple or ornate. For me, entertaining is creative expression, every bit as inventive as decorating or designing a landscape. Hosting parties brings me joy from the second an event is on the calendar to the moment the last guest walks out the door; I adore creating exquisite memories for my family and friends to share. So however exhausted I may find myself by the end of the evening, I am still smiling, knowing I've given all a night to remember.

Planning parties didn't always come naturally to me. I grew up in a red-brick Tudor house not far from my current home in Los Angeles, where, as a child, I was shy and clung to my mother's leg at social engagements. My earliest memories of festivities at our house include perfumed ladies in beehive hairdos and flowing silk Halston dresses; the men, strong and stoic, in dark suits with glasses of scotch in hand. My social butterfly parents entertained constantly, from formal dinners at our dining table with long flickering candles, to my debutante party, to Bobby Short playing the piano in our garden at my dad's sixtieth birthday party. Mother was beautiful and glamorous; Father strong, mannerly, and intellectual. They seemed perfect, and so did their parties.

It wasn't until I was older that I learned that parties aren't about perfection, but joy. Of course, it took some time for me to get here, and I made my share of mistakes. When I was newly married, my husband and I entertained very simply; I had two or three go-to dishes—Cornish game hen, Caesar salad, and a berry cobbler recipe from my sister. One night, I held a dinner party in our library, the table beautifully set with china, flowers, and flickering candles—but no napkins! Another evening, our dinner party strolled into the garden for after-dinner drinks in the evening air and I walked back into the house to get something from the kitchen. I spotted our late cocker spaniel, Norman, with all four paws on the dining room table, slurping up the leftovers before they'd been cleared! The more I entertained, the more I gained confidence and learned that snafus are what bring humor and authenticity to the moment.

My home offices are well-stocked with beautiful monogrammed stationery
in different colors and my favorite black-ink pens. After attending events,
I love to follow up with handwritten thank you notes for a personal touch.

"I'm going to make everything around me beautiful—that will be my life." — *Elsie de Wolfe*

As our kids got older, I found myself with more time on my hands, and a bounty of friends and family with whom we wanted to spend quality time. Planning and hosting parties became one of my favorite extracurriculars. After all those years, I finally knew why my parents loved entertaining so! Events are a gift—both from your guests, who take the time show up for you, and for them, in the form of a special experience. Guests should feel welcome and comfortable and enjoy a celebration that is a reflection of your personality and verve. The magic comes when you have created a setting where beauty can unfold. I'm not just referring to literal beauty (the tabletop décor, the photogenic hors d'oeuvre) but the intangible: the laughter and friendship shared.

I eventually found my own voice and my own way of entertaining. I've learned there is a strength in staying true to your own vision while being inspired by others. I don't get caught up in the latest fads, but I do use the world around me for inspiration.

Almost all of the parties in this book were hosted at home, as that's my favorite place to entertain. Time with family and friends is our greatest luxury. When I renovated my home in Los Angeles with the help of designer Jeffrey Bilhuber, I asked him to help me carve out specific areas for entertaining. We created an outdoor loggia that faces our garden and is heated by both a fireplace and ceiling heaters so we can enjoy it year-round. We also designed a larger bar, loosely inspired by the one at the Carlyle Hotel in New York, with a cozy banquette that you can curl up on for cocktails and camaraderie.

Something I have discovered over the years is that the planning process is part of the fun. I spend as many careful hours plotting out a garden dinner as some couples spend on planning their wedding celebrations! I have a pinboard in my office for organizing my plans, and, of course, a multitude of Pinterest boards for gathering ideas. It's all about quantity, in the beginning: as with anything, you start out with twenty ideas and then simplify it and hone it until there is a cohesiveness to the party plan. I spend the most time on seating arrangements, because connections and conversation are vital to a party's success. My other area of focus is the palette. I see the world in color. I like to carry a color palette throughout, from the flowers to the food to my outfit. There's nothing like first impressions, and when guests walk in I want them to be wowed—not by extravagance, but by the setting.

Set a pretty bowl on your desk to gather invitations for design inspiration. Fresh flowers always brighten my day.

I prefer to keep my letter-writing necessities close at hand—such as on a pretty silver tray on my desktop. OPPOSITE: White anemones are one of my favorite flowers: simple and sophisticated.

It's important to visualize your party as a guest will experience it, and doing so gives me a chance to make any needed tweaks long beforehand. I like to say an event is like a play: it has a first, second and third act. We've all been to parties where the line for the bar was too long, or there weren't enough appetizers being passed. For this reason, I like to approach my parties like a director, thinking through every single detail. I imagine everything from start to finish—from greeting the guests upon arrival to walking the last guest out the door. I stroll through the different rooms in our home, considering what the experience will be like. And of course, I triple-check that our menu will satisfy them; we never want a guest running to In-N-Out after dining at our house.

The day of the party, I find that there is an electrifying feeling in the air in the moments before my first guest arrives. There is a bit of a rush every hostess knows well—I get dressed, adjust the place settings, turn on the music, and make sure to have a cocktail in-hand to set the tone. I hope this book transports you and inspires you to create your own magic. Open your doors, and your hearts, and entertain!

The Essentials

or me, the joy of entertaining is in the details: coordinating the colors, selecting the china, choosing the linens, and having it all come to fruition seamlessly. No detail is too small! To orchestrate a dreamy event, I focus on a few necessities that, when combined, create a fête to remember. These include elegant invitations to set the tone, bounteous flowers, an in-season menu, and tablescapes that do more than serve: they delight the eyes. Read on for more advice you will want to keep in your back pocket—though you'll want to tailor it to your own creative process over time. Happy planning!

INSPIRATION

A party's theme, or purpose, is where it all begins for me. If you determine the party's modus operandi far in advance, it sets the tone for all decisions to follow. Is this an elegant seated dinner, a luncheon buffet, or a cocktail party? Once you know what you are working toward, it will guide all the rest of your decisions and make planning much simpler.

My favorite type of party is a couples dinner party, because it is so intimate and inspires so many real friendships and great conversations. I also love a beautiful garden party—as a California girl, I love entertaining outside. I am also always looking for an excuse to dance the night away, so great music or even a DJ is requisite. No matter what theme you select, remember this: the point is to have fun.

To find my color palette for the event, I often start with a very simple idea. Perhaps I'm inspired by a flower, a fabric, a time of year, or a special occasion. Follow your passions. After all, this is a way to express yourself—if you are inspired, your guests will be inspired. Once I select my theme and palette, I run with it, using it to guide all decisions about invitations, décor, and entertainment. I utilize both a Pinterest board and a physical pinboard in my office to keep everything organized and in one spot. There are no boundaries— anything and everything related to the theme is added, whether it is inspiration from nature, architecture, fashion, jewelry, travel, or food. As I'm planning, I keep returning to these guiding lights to help me brainstorm.

Remaining consistent in your theme and capitalizing upon it with an abundance of repetition, as I did for a blue and white (and pink!) charity luncheon on my loggia, is the most effective way to cast a spell as a hostess.

INVITATIONS

Invitations don't need to be elaborate, but they do need to be informative. Include as much detail as possible to put your guests at ease. What's the purpose of the party? Whether it's an elegant cocktail hour or poolside pizza, be sure that's reflected in the invites. Go beyond address and time to give other helpful necessary information, i.e., whether it's a seated dinner, passed hors d'oeuvre, or a buffet. We all find comfort in a bit of fashion direction. The more information you can share with your guests in advance, the more comfortable they'll be. No one relishes being over- or under-dressed! A few of my favorite expressions I've used as prompts: "Guys, No Ties"; "City Chic"; and "Bold and Bright."

For special events, such as a fiftieth birthday or a wedding, I send a save-the-date four months in advance and send mailed invitations at least eight weeks in advance, especially if guests need to make travel arrangements. Receiving an invitation in the mail is thrilling, and a must for major events. I love engraved invitations on thick card stock from Aardvark Letterpress in Los Angeles or Willow Papery in Sun Valley, Idaho. For more casual gatherings, I use e-vites from Paperless Post, which I find the most reliable. I like that you can confirm receipt and make the guest list public or private. Just remember, the invitation sets the tone of the party, reinforces the theme, and creates excitement for the festivity that awaits. Match the tone of the event to the invite, and you'll begin making magic as soon as they open the envelope, real or virtual!

The invitation you select makes your event's first impression. Be sure it is as exquisite as your party will be with the assistance of calligraphed lettering, embossed illustrations, and sheer overlays.

FLOWERS

Nurture your relationship with your local florist as you would tend a garden. Weeks before any party, I stop by my local flower market to reserve the blooms I want in advance. Peonies, garden roses, anemones, ranunculus, mums, viburnum, and hydrangeas are consistently a safe bet. Expand upon the color palette of your home so everything coordinates. Occasionally I'll combine various types of flowers, but it's much more common for me to do one color or blossom— a lush and dramatic look. However, I don't like arrangements to look overdone. There should be a naturalness to flowers, as if you've collected them from the garden that morning.

Abundance and repetition are the secret to a coherent flower plan—you may wish to do a trio of low vases down a long table, or gather large ones on an adjacent sideboard for a theatrical moment. I also love to work with topiaries, wheatgrass, and citrus like lemons, limes, and kumquats, which can add so much interest to an arrangement. Using a variety of containers as vases makes the arrangement more appealing to the eye. Everything from mercury glass to etched crystal to antique silver will work.

To keep floral stress at bay, create your arrangements the day before, so the blooms have time to open up and become the lushest versions of themselves. Cut each stem at an angle with shearing scissors before setting it in your vessel of choice. I keep my flower arrangements in the wine cellar overnight to preserve them before each party, but any chilly area (even the refrigerator) will do. Another trick to keep them fresh: include a bit of vodka or 7 Up to the water to give each stem a little pep.

Select seasonal flowers for the freshest possible effect, and remember that there is strength in numbers. Sometimes, a steady row of blooms is more impactful than one large bouquet in the center of a table. FOLLOWING PAGE: I am continually adding to my collection of cocktail napkins. You never know when a party's theme will call for an embroidered monogram—or an embroidered monkey!

TABLESCAPE

Like an architect surveying a landscape before beginning to draw floor plans, you must know what type of table you'll be working with before you can effectively strategize for an event. Are you doing a seated dinner in your dining room, a larger-scale event with rentals, or an afternoon picnic in your garden under the shade of a jacaranda tree? Once you select the setting for your table, you can begin planning your tablescape.

The beauty of a tablescape is based on the myriad pieces—the flowers, china, linens, and silver—that make up the whole. If I'm hosting outside in the loggia, I select china and linens that coordinate with the garden, perhaps in green or blue-and-white to complement the surrounding chinoiserie porcelain. Over the years, I've purchased and inherited china—L'Objet, Ginori, Herend—that harmonizes with the hues of our décor. One of my secrets is to use buffet plates as dinner plates—because they're larger and flatter than the norm, I think food looks prettier on them. As you accessorize your tabletop, know that

it's fine to mix metals, such as gold and silver, but you may want to include votives in mercury glass—which reads as both—to tie it all together. There has to be a cohesiveness to the story of the event that you carry throughout.

When you're indoors, it's all about using your tablescape to harmonize with the adjacent color palette and décor of your home and not distract from it. As when applying makeup, the goal is to make it a prettier version of itself—not garish. I make my table a reflection of the time of year and the purpose of the event and always prefer it to look organic rather than fussy. Keep flowers low, so they do not impede conversation across the table. You want your décor to complement the party, not compete with it.

If you are hosting outdoors, it can be a nice touch to place pashminas on women's chairs in colors that coordinate with the party's theme. Every table should have lots of candles flickering—candlelight is inviting, creates an atmosphere of celebration, and, best of all, makes your guests look their most radiant (which will make them feel radiant, too).

LINENS

I've long adored beautiful table linens. I inherited some from my mother that I cherish, and over the years I have slowly added new items from my travels. These range from unadorned woven placemats to intricately monogrammed linens that reflect the colors of our dining room. My sources include Talmaris in Paris, Julia B., Deborah Sharpe, New Orleans–based Leontine Linens, and Halo Home by KSW. I have such fun with my stockpile of cocktail napkins, embroidered in a wide variety of riotously fun themes that reflect my passions—from dragonflies to topiaries to monograms. Because cocktail napkins are literally in your guests' hands, they provide a smart place to add a dose of humor! Don't take yourself too seriously.

For the dining room, I have a few sets of table

linens for parties of twelve people in various shapes—rectangular, oval, octagonal, round. If you're just beginning your collection, it's nice to start with classic white rectangular hemstitch linens as a basic set. Then, if you want to add a color go for green—green goes with everything. Look around at the colors in your dining room and keep them in mind when purchasing your linens—you may even want to have a photo of the room on your phone so you can color-match while you're shopping.

In my storage cabinets, I separate my linens by level of formality so that they are highly organized—I can quickly pull out what I need to use for any type of event. Put tissue paper between sets of placemats and linens so they're well-ordered. The easier it is for you to eyeball your choices, the better the selections you'll make.

SEATING

When you are planning a seating chart, it is wise to separate couples. The magic lies in conversations unfolding and friendships being made, and those things happen far less frequently when spouses are seated next to each other. (Then, at the end of the evening, spouses can reconnect and enjoy sharing their unique experiences with their dinner partners.) As hosts, my husband, Steve, and I often divide and conquer: we'll each sit at opposite ends of the room or table, so we're both on duty to ensure good conversation and connections among our guests.

I prefer men and women to be intermixed evenly and often seat a guest next to one person they know and one they don't know. I'll think about possible connections they might share—perhaps a city they share in common, a philanthropic connection, or a school they both attended. Life is about one degree of separation, and when a guest sits down at one of our dinner parties they should know they are seated with purpose and must have something in common with their neighbor. I am also a fan of mixing generations—we all learn from one another; it's fun to pass on wisdom and to receive it as well. I'll often have our teenagers and twenty-something kids invite their friends to bring increased energy and variety to the party.

Planning a dinner party's seating arrangements is one of the most important tasks of a hostess. Do it right, and you may create new friendships that last a lifetime. FOLLOWING PAGE: My husband, Steve, regaling the crowd as the ultimate toastmaster.

FOOD

One of my favorite phrases is "food is décor." It's absolutely true—so by all means, make your menu choices beautiful and colorful! Seasonality is also key when it comes to selecting your menu. It is essential to be authentic as a hostess, and to that end, I would rather serve a really good simple salad with fresh-picked lettuce from a farmer's market, or a cheese soufflé, than something contrived. Opt for flavorful over fussy: simple dishes are underrated. Some of my appetizers of choice are relatively uncomplicated: ahi tuna tartar on wonton wrappers, smoked salmon blinis, and miniature duck quesadillas. A mix of high and low is unquestionably delicious.

Plan a menu that helps, rather than hinders, socializing. Keep passed hors d'oeuvre bite-sized and easy to eat. Avoid greens and other foods that get caught in teeth. I always prefer to pre-slice meat, too, so no one needs to grapple with sharp knives at the table. And it should go without saying: avoid overly garlic-laden dishes. My rule of thumb is to limit the dishes to small portions with no heavy sauces.

Develop relationships with a few caterers in your city, because you will find they each have different strengths. Some are experts at large-scale formal events; others ideal for a quiet evening at home with friends. I work with my chosen caterer to plan the menu for each event at least a few weeks in advance (earlier for large-scale parties), so that if we run into any issues sourcing seasonal food, we know as soon as possible. If you have time, it's wise to do a tasting dinner—especially if you're planning a large event. That way you can make sure the appetizers are the correct size, easy to eat, don't fall apart, and so on. If I am planning an intimate dinner, I reach out to my guests well beforehand to inquire about any food allergies. The night of the event, I make sure to have a chat with the staff before everyone arrives, thanking them for being there and making them feel good so they do their jobs well. Our goal is to pamper every single guest and encourage them to let go and enjoy!

THE BAR

Always maintain a full bar, so you're able to enjoy whatever you like at any point. In addition to our liquors of choice, which I display on beautiful silver trays atop the bar, I keep my refrigerator stocked with mini individual bottles of San Pellegrino, tonic water, cranberry juice, and Sprite, so nothing is wasted.

Always have a variety of glassware at the ready: lowball, martini, wine, and Champagne glasses. Together, they create a hospitable display. I always make sure the bar itself is super clean, with one linen bar towel out so the bartender can wipe their hands. You want it to look not like a workspace, but like a beautiful continuation of your home. Near my bar I always keep a little bowl of nuts—See's Candies' mixed salted nuts are the best in the world—and drawers of festive nibbles like truffle potato chips and popcorn.

A GOOD HOSTESS

- Welcomes you into her world.
- Is always ready fifteen minutes early.
- Is relaxed, with a cocktail in hand, when she greets you.
- Has a warm embrace and a smile on her face.
- Has a positive, enthusiastic attitude.
- Makes it look effortless.
- Is unfazed by hiccups large or small.
- Creates a diverse guest list.
- Goes high and low with both food and décor.
- Doesn't take herself too seriously.
- Always has a toast on the tip of her tongue.
- Has a merry time, and is as delighted to be there as her guests are.

A GOOD GUEST

- Brings energy, charm, and a small hostess gift.

- Arrives ten minutes late and recognizes when the party is winding down.

- Mingles and meets all, not just longtime friends.

- Engages the person to the right and to the left at the dinner table.

- Is well-versed in current events.

- Has a positive, enthusiastic attitude and, of course, a sense of humor.

- Is self-sufficient, not needy.

- Isn't nosy and doesn't open your cabinets.

- Isn't the first one to run out the door.

- Writes a thank-you note.

- Is one you can't wait to invite back.

A Housewarming Cocktail Party

There is no nicer invitation in the world than being asked into someone's home. A housewarming is the perfect opportunity to do just that for your friends, who will no doubt adore seeing your new residence.

Ultimately, the people make the party, but designing a home that's tailored specifically for entertaining contributes to the success of every event you'll host there. If you have friends and family over as frequently as we do, it's essential. When my husband Steve and I got married, our new large, blended family consisted of seven children of various ages. To kick off our new life together properly, we wanted to create a home that would provide space enough for our children and ourselves, function beautifully on a day-to-day level, and welcome a wide array of friends into our newly combined lives.

PARTY INSPIRATION:
OUR NEW HOME

PALETTE:
AMETHYST, PERIDOT, CHOCOLATE,
GOLD, AND IVORY

FLOWERS:
GREEN HYDRANGEAS,
BRIGHT PINK PEONIES, TANGERINE AND
PURPLE CALLA LILIES, TULIPS

TABLETOP ELEMENTS:
GILDED GOLD AND SILVER TRAYS;
DRAGONFLY COCKTAIL NAPKINS

FOOD & DRINK:
A SOPHISTICATED SPREAD
OF FINGER FOODS

Our 1951 house was designed by legendary Hollywood Regency architect John Elgin Woolf. Each of his properties is a Slim Aarons photograph sprung to life—think mansard roofs, an abundance of French doors leading to gardens, pool houses, and calming symmetry. There was so much to love about our house, and together my husband and I wanted to make it our own.

Enter designer Jeffrey Bilhuber. What I love about Jeffrey's work—beyond his brilliant design skills—is his vision for creating numerous seating areas within one home, which promotes intimate conversation. He added cocktail tables that can be easily moved for each particular party's needs, and low lighting that glamorizes guests and puts everyone in a festive mood the moment they walk in.

After Jeffrey transformed our interiors, we hosted an elegant open house cocktail soirée for a grand reveal. I decided guests would gather in our central living room. Jeffrey had designed it in captivating jewel tones—deep amethyst and peridot—that sparked a color palette of equally saturated hues. From there, the party could spill over into the adjacent library and bar, where lacquered dark chocolate walls are so very rich.

Over the years, I've cultivated a relationship with my local flower market, so I called them well in advance to ensure they would have blooms in stock that would help me build the visual effect I sought—orange tulips, raspberry peonies, purple calla lilies—and match Jeffrey's design. In the days before the event, I devised a playlist for the evening—songs like "Heart of Glass" by The Puppini Sisters and Vance Joy's "Riptide" created a rolicking atmosphere. (When I need inspiration, Tory Burch's playlists on Spotify are my go-to for cocktail party music.) That night, I encouraged guests to wander and explore, while we kept cocktails and appetizers flowing constantly, as people continued to stroll in and out of the open house.

I chose to serve various easy-to-eat nibbles that reflected the colors of our central living room and library bar, like lobster soup that echoed the hues of the leopard upholstery in the library. Crudités were offered in Moroccan tea tumblers that matched the plush aubergine velvet sofas adjacent to the roaring fire. When you put care into the little details you cast a spell and create indelible memories, which is what entertaining at home is all about.

Bundling the freshest possible blooms creates a stunning place for the eye to land; arranging them in loose bouquets imparts an organic vibe. Here, green hydrangeas highlight green and black zebra-striped velvet on the adjacent side chairs. FOLLOWING PAGES: Dark pink peonies reflect the jewel-toned décor.

Place blooms around the
room in bud vases so guests
find beauty at every angle.

THIS PAGE: Vary the sizes and colors of trays and bowls to create visual interest on your table; decorate platters with bay leaves, rosemary, tangerine slices, and the like for Instagrammable allure. OPPOSITE: I selected gold-rimmed trays and dishes to echo the surrounding gilded furniture.

OPPOSITE: I always
include a wide variety
of *fromage*—soft and
hard—on my charcuterie
and cheese platters so there's
something for everyone. Adding
fruit and olives creates nice balance.
THIS PAGE: Using colorful Moroccan tea glasses
on a silver tray creates a transportive serving solution
for rainbow-hued crudités and beet hummus.

OPPOSITE: A few of our go-to tipples: Grey Goose and Belvedere vodka, Macallan scotch, Patron Silver Tequila (for margaritas), and Jose Cuervo Reserva de la Familia tequila (for sipping).

THIS PAGE: The chocolate lacquered walls of our library and bar transport guests to the dark, storied bars of London and New York—everything and everyone seems to glimmer brighter against the dark backdrop.

OPPOSITE: Our signature cocktail: pomegranate-grapefruit cosmopolitans with pink grapefruit sugared rims and orange peels. THIS PAGE: Jeffrey Bilhuber lined the library's built-in bar with mirrors that maximize light; my collection of Murano glassware adds a note of colorful fun.

I believe in letting flowers be themselves. Tulips have a dancer's wild grace—why hem them in? In tangerine orange, these particular blooms complement the leopard upholstery in the library and echo the linen napkins and the lobster soup, served in Calvin Klein pewter teacups.

POMEGRANATE-GRAPEFRUIT COSMOPOLITAN

Cosmopolitans brightened with fresh
in-season pomegranates.
Makes 12 drinks

½ cup sugar
6 cups fresh pomegranate seeds
3 cups ruby red grapefruit vodka, such as Absolut
1 ½ cups freshly squeezed lime juice
Ice
1 batch Pink Grapefruit Sugar
12 ¾ x 3-inch strips fresh orange peel

Combine the 1/2 cup sugar with 1 cup water in a
saucepan and simmer until the sugar has dissolved;
cool syrup. Puree the pomegranate seeds in a blender,
pulsing just until the juice is released. Strain the juice
through a sieve into a bowl, pressing on the seeds and
pulp. Mix the pomegranate juice, vodka, lime juice,
and just enough of the syrup to sweeten to taste in a
large pitcher. Chill up to 4 hours. Add ice to the
pitcher and stir well to chill, then strain into glasses
rimmed with Pink Grapefruit Sugar and garnish each
with a strip of orange peel.

PINK GRAPEFRUIT SUGAR

1 pink grapefruit
3 tablespoons sugar

Using a microplane, grate 1 tablespoon of zest. Mix the
zest with the sugar on a small plate. Cut a wedge from
the grapefruit and run it around the rim of 12 martini
glasses. Dip rims in sugar.

CRUDITÉ CUPS WITH BEET HUMMUS

This classic hummus gets a boost of color and flavor
from roasted beets.
Serves 8 to 12

2 medium beets (about 7 ounces), roasted
1 ½ teaspoons extra-virgin olive oil,
    plus 2 tablespoons reserved
1 15-ounce can garbanzo beans, rinsed and drained
¼ cup freshly squeezed lemon juice
2 tablespoons tahini
2 cloves garlic
¾ teaspoon sea salt
Assorted crudités, such as baby carrots, Persian
    cucumbers, fennel, and bell peppers, cut into julienne
Fresh dill sprigs

Preheat the oven to 400°F. Place the beets in a small
baking dish and drizzle with 1 ½ teaspoons of the oil.
Cover with foil and bake until the beets are tender
when pierced with a paring knife. Cool completely.
Trim, peel, and quarter the beets. Combine the beets,
garbanzo beans, lemon juice, the remaining tahini,
the remaining 2 tablespoons olive oil, garlic, and salt
in a food processor fitted with the metal blade and
process into a smooth puree.

Place 2 to 3 tablespoons of hummus in individual
cups. Arrange the crudité and dill in the cups on top
of the hummus and serve.

Pick up lobster bisque at your favorite seafood restaurant and embellish it with crème fraîche, lobster, and tarragon for an artful dish that's nearly too pretty to eat.

OPPOSITE: Look for cocktail napkins that evoke your personality—I have some with monkeys, others with dragonflies, and even a few with the words Tequila, Whiskey, Cognac. Don't take them too seriously! THIS PAGE: A long banquette is ideal for parties, because it encourages mixing and movement; metallic wallpaper gives guests a glow.

Bring dessert trays out toward the end of the evening to give guests a sweet send-off and signify that the party is winding down. Here, on a three-tiered tray, cookies are paired with panna cotta infused with rosewater tea, a traditional beverage I imported from my travels in the Middle East.

"Life is a party. Dress like it." —Lilly Pulitzer

WELCOMING STYLE

WHEN YOU'RE HOSTING AN EVENT in your home, align your wardrobe for the night with the colors in your interiors, the food, and flowers.

LOOK AROUND FOR INSPIRATION, and let the rooms you'll be using for entertaining give you ideas for flowers, food, and décor. It's an approach that always works, whether you have a modern house that's more neutral or a traditional one that's filled with radiant color.

IT'S ALWAYS FUN to have a signature cocktail at the beginning of the night, especially one that nods to the theme of the evening. Make it a reflection of something

that's important to you, the hostess—perhaps your spouse's favorite vodka.

ENTERTAINING AT HOME, I tend to focus on what I'm wearing above the waist, as that's what people notice most. Think statement earrings, a fun necklace, or a beautiful blouse. And I *always* feel more festive in heels.

STEVE AND I LIKE TO MAKE SURE our outfits complement each other. It sets the tone for the party, after all! And he's a good sport about it.

WHEN YOU, AS THE HOSTESS, get dressed up, it sets the tone instantly.

One of my fashion philosophies is that what you wear from the waist up is most important, so I always don big earrings or a statement necklace. A woman feels more feminine in heels, so they're a must, as are loose, non-constrictive blouses.

A Ladies' Charity Luncheon

Last spring, I hadn't seen a few of my girlfriends in a while, and was trying to think of an excuse for us to get together. It's so important for women to support other women's endeavors that I decided this lunch should be in support of a charity. It takes a village—all of us!—to empower one another. Thrive Animal Rescue, a California-based dog rescue, was started by a dear friend, Georgia Spogli; it places abused and abandoned dogs in their forever homes. At the luncheon, a generous percentage of all purchases from our friend Anne Sisteron's beautiful jewelry collection would benefit Thrive.

PARTY INSPIRATION:
A LUSH SPRINGTIME GARDEN

PALETTE:
BLUSH PINK, SKY BLUE, AND CRISP WHITE

FLOWERS:
PINK LILACS, TULIPS, SWEET PEAS,
ROSES, AND GREEN VIBURNUM
IN CHINOISERIE VASES AND BUD VASES

TABLETOP ELEMENTS:
SPRING GREEN CHARGERS;
BLUE AND WHITE HEREND CHINA;
PAISLEY TABLECLOTH; TOPIARY BOXWOOD
BALLS; BLUE CRYSTAL BUTTERFLIES

FOOD & DRINK:
SALADS, TEA SANDWICHES, AND CAKES

———————

Anne and I have been close for twenty years, since our children started school together. I've always been inspired by both the colors and the stones she uses in her creations. I'm a huge fan of her earrings and often wear them when traveling to exotic locations. Anne started her business when her boys were young. A decade later, both her boys and her business have grown significantly.

The color palette that afternoon was one of my all-time favorites—blue and white—the exact colors of cumulus clouds rolling in a California sky. Our loggia is the perfect showcase for all the chinoiserie I've collected over the years—blue and white coordinates seamlessly with the exuberant green of a garden. I used a paisley fabric as a custom tablecloth to set beneath my family collection of Herend Rothschild Bird china. It beautifully complemented a menu of colorful salads (including chicken and wild greens Caesar salad and a nasturtium-dotted shrimp and asparagus salad), prosciutto and aged gouda sandwiches, and a spring pea soup. We sipped rosé—of course, you have to serve rosé at a ladies' luncheon!—shopped for Anne's jewelry, mingled, and then sat down to a beautiful lunch.

The tablecloth's swirling motif formed a graphic backdrop for the floral arrangements: bursting pink lilacs, French tulips, sweet peas, roses, and viburnum. Porcelain ginger jars became vases for the event, containing a riot of pink variegated hydrangeas, green hydrangeas, and blush tulips on a sideboard and forming a bountiful backdrop for the luncheon; I set complementary blue and white chinoiserie bud vases on the tablescape. Topiaries are a go-to for me. I've always been a fan of them for both interior and exterior parties because they're so classic and balance the fussiness of floral arrangements. All the greenery brought the adjacent garden into the loggia. Blue crystal butterflies rested atop easy-to-maintain dried boxwood balls above each set plate on the tabletop, extending the springtime theme.

As my girlfriends and I chatted and sat sipping rosé, our happiness at being together was enhanced by the knowledge that the afternoon would benefit Thrive.

Blue and white chinoiserie pops in our loggia, thanks to the expanse of lush green plantings beyond. FOLLOWING PAGES: Arranging flowers at various heights echoes the natural lines of a garden and encourages the eye to wander.

OPPOSITE: Dotting the table with lithe little bud vases set around larger flower arrangements gives every guest proximity to garden grandeur. THIS PAGE, CLOCKWISE FROM LEFT: A tablescape is more than flowers, china, and linens—even your place card holders should be eye candy. For this al fresco luncheon, I set the table with some of the most spring-like china in my collection, including the Herend Rothschild Bird with Blue Border and my inherited green buffet plates. FOLLOWING PAGES: Twinkly Baccarat butterflies captivated atop preserved boxwood balls at each place setting for a bit of whimsy. I typically use one type of flower per vase, but the season's sweet peas, hydrangeas, garden roses, and more begged for their own get-together.

PREVIOUS PAGES: Jeffrey Bilhuber created
symmetry in the loggia reflective of both our
home and the garden beyond the columns.
THIS PAGE: Selecting blooms in one color
palette leads to a cohesive look. CLOCKWISE
FROM LEFT: Ranunculus, hyacinth, lilacs.
OPPOSITE: The loggia's fireplace and outdoor
heaters allow for constant comfort.

THESE PAGES: Is there anything more ladylike than flowers? Bring them into a luncheon in an unexpected way by topping dishes with edible blooms, such as the nasturtium-dotted shrimp and asparagus salad with forbidden rice in the foreground. FOLLOWING PAGE, LEFT: Serving light, easy to eat, and colorful fare is recommended at a ladies' luncheon so everyone feels her best. FOLLOWING PAGE, RIGHT, CLOCKWISE FROM TOP RIGHT: Oro blanco grapefruit, cara cara orange, kiwi, and kumquat salad with mint; avocado, smoked trout, hearts of palm, and watermelon radish slices on crisps with yuzu drizzle; prosciutto and aged gouda sandwiches and mini egg salad sandwiches.

THE MENU

ROSÉ

SPRING PEA SOUP WITH CRÈME FRAÎCHE,
MICROGREENS, AND EDIBLE FLOWER PETALS

SHRIMP AND ASPARAGUS SALAD
WITH FORBIDDEN RICE

AVOCADO, SMOKED TROUT,
HEARTS OF PALM, AND WATERMELON RADISHES
ON CRISPS WITH YUZU DRIZZLE

ORO BLANCO GRAPEFRUIT, CARA CARA ORANGE,
KIWI, AND KUMQUAT SALAD WITH MINT

CHICKEN CAESAR SALAD

MINI EGG SALAD SANDWICHES AND PROSCIUTTO
AND AGED GOUDA SANDWICHES

VANILLA LAYER CAKE WITH RED BERRY
PRESERVES AND VANILLA BUTTERCREAM

RASPBERRY, PISTACHIO,
AND BLACKBERRY MACARONS

MILK CHOCOLATE TRUFFLES WITH
CANDIED ROSE PETALS

SHRIMP AND ASPARAGUS SALAD WITH FORBIDDEN RICE AND NASTURTIUMS

Have your fishmonger peel and cook large fancy shrimp to top this colorful salad. Forbidden rice, also known as black rice, is both flavorful and rich in antioxidants.
Serves 6

Sea salt
12 ounces asparagus, trimmed
⅓ cup freshly squeezed lemon juice
1 tablespoon honey
1 small shallot, minced
½ teaspoon sea salt, plus more for asparagus water
⅓ cup extra-virgin olive oil
¾ cup forbidden rice
12 cooked, peeled, and deveined jumbo shrimp
Nasturtium flowers for garnish

Fill a 10- or 12-inch skillet with enough water to come 1 inch up the sides; season with a pinch of salt. Bring the water to a boil. Add the asparagus, cover, and simmer until the asparagus is crisp-tender, about 2 minutes. Drain and plunge into ice water to cool and refresh. Drain the asparagus well.

Whisk the lemon juice, honey, shallot, and ½ teaspoon salt in a small bowl to blend. Gradually whisk in the olive oil and set the dressing aside.

Place the rice, 3 cups water, and a pinch of salt in a heavy medium saucepan and bring to a boil. Reduce the heat to low, cover, and simmer until the rice is tender and has absorbed the liquid, about 50 minutes. Transfer the rice to a medium bowl and cool completely. Add half of the dressing to the rice and stir to combine.

Arrange the rice in the center of a platter and top with asparagus and shrimp. Spoon the remaining dressing over the shrimp and asparagus. Garnish with nasturtiums.

SPRING PEA AND WATERCRESS SOUP WITH GREEN ONIONS AND CRÈME FRAÎCHE

A vibrant green and rich with spring favorites, such as peas, watercress, and green onions, this soup is the perfect first course for a formal luncheon, especially when garnished with crème fraîche, microgreens, and edible flowers.
Serves 6

1 tablespoon extra-virgin olive oil
⅔ cup sliced green onions
2 cloves garlic, chopped
1 teaspoon grated fresh ginger
5 cups chicken broth
1 8-ounce russet potato, peeled and cut into 1-inch pieces
4 cups watercress leaves
3 cups freshly shelled peas, or 1 pound frozen peas
⅓ cup crème fraîche, plus more for garnish
Salt and freshly ground white pepper to taste
Microgreens and edible flowers for garnish

Heat the olive oil in a heavy large saucepan over medium-high heat. Add the green onions, garlic, and ginger and sauté until the green onion is tender, about 1 minute. Add the broth and the potato and bring to a simmer. Cover and cook over medium heat until the potato is very tender, about 12 minutes. Stir in the watercress and peas. Cover and cook until the peas are tender, about 4 minutes. Cool slightly. Purée the soup in batches in a blender. Return the soup to the saucepan and whisk in the ⅓ cup crème fraîche. Season the soup to taste with salt and pepper. (The soup can be prepared up to 3 days ahead. Cover and refrigerate.)

Reheat the soup by stirring over medium heat until the soup just simmers. Ladle the soup into bowls and garnish with additional crème fraîche, microgreens, and edible flowers.

THIS PAGE: I like to provide myriad dessert options so every guest feels taken care of. In this case that means milk chocolate truffles with candied rose petals; raspberry, pistachio, and blackberry macarons; and a vanilla layer cake with red berry preserves and vanilla buttercream. OPPOSITE: Varying the height of display stands make the desserts look even more divine.

THIS PAGE, CLOCKWISE FROM TOP LEFT: In my rose garden, we selected soft blush and taupe-hued blooms that would complement each other. The Heritage rose by David Austin Roses has a transcendent fruit-and-honey fragrance. Heritage, Koko Loko, Winchester Cathedral, and Bolero roses have all the grandeur of couture ball gowns. OPPOSITE: A pair of tulipieres put fresh-cut blooms on proud display.

"It's not what you put on the table, it's who you put in the chairs." —Betsy Bloomingdale

PARTIES WITH A PURPOSE

PHILANTHROPY IS REALLY IMPORTANT to me. Nothing makes me happier than combining my love of entertaining with purposeful charity. Large or small, entertaining for charity is a wonderful way to give back.

THERE ARE ENDLESS WAYS to host a charitable event—consider a book signing with an author, a jewelry or clothing show that supports a friend's line, or a luncheon or large-scale dinner to benefit charities in your community.

LET YOUR GUESTS KNOW that the event will be benefiting the cause of your choice on the invitation so they come prepared to shop or donate.

IT'S OFTEN NICE TO CHOOSE A CHARITY that has a connection with your community, such as one that supports local schools, hospitals, museums, or the arts.

TO CREATE YOUR GUEST LIST, reach out and gather a group of friends who share a passion for certain charities, or those with similar interests.

CHARITY EVENTS don't have to be large. Even an intimate one can make a difference.

Baubles by my friend, jewelry designer Anne Sisteron, inspired generous giving to Thrive Animal Rescue.

A Gentlemen's Wine and Cigar Party

Giving someone you love their own party, fully orchestrated, up to and including lighting the candles—without attending it yourself—can be great fun. It's one of my favorite ways to give back to my husband, Steve. In this instance, I wanted to honor Steve's passion for wine. What could be a more perfect present than planning a men's evening at our home in Los Angeles where he and his friends could enjoy big, juicy steaks with some of his favorite red wines?

PARTY INSPIRATION:
MEN AND WINE

PALETTE:
BURGUNDY, TEAL, AND GOLD

FLOWERS:
PURPLE HELLEBORES AND AMARANTHUS IN TALL VASES AND AN ANTIQUE TUREEN

TABLETOP ELEMENTS:
A CUT-VELVET TABLECLOTH IN TEAL AND METALLIC CHOCOLATE; FEATHER-TOPPED ANTIQUE SILVER CIGAR PLATES WITH FEATHERS; GOLD NAPKINS WITH CLEAN-LINED SILVER NAPKIN RINGS; TOWERING GOLD AND BURGUNDY TAPER CANDLES

FOOD & DRINK:
STEAKHOUSE SPLENDOR

That evening, Steve's wines of choice were from BOND, founded in Napa Valley by Bill Harlan and Bob Levy. This portfolio of wines creates Grand Cru–quality Cabernet Sauvignon from five small vineyards—each between seven and eleven acres in size—that it helps manage, all under the umbrella of one team, with one singular vision. I love that BOND was named for Harlan's mother. The wine labels are evocative of old bank notes, which added a historic touch to the table that seemed perfectly suited to the meal.

The tablescape was inspired by the great New York restaurants of the Gilded Age, such as Delmonico's. I used gilded plates, a cut-velvet tablecloth, and moody, manly flowers: purple hellebores and amaranthus that dangled over my grandmother's antique silver tureen. Down the middle of the long table, gold candlesticks (a gift to me from Steve) in an array of heights held burgundy and gold tapers like bulwarks.

After a fun cocktail hour, Steve and his friends sat down to feast on a photogenic yet masculine menu, including beet and blue cheese salads, dry-aged porterhouse steaks cooked on a salt block, and pommes frites with garlic aioli and ketchup. For dessert: black and tan sundaes with homemade hot fudge and caramel sauce and gilt truffles provided a kick for the post-dinner course of cigar smoking and whiskey.

Because he loves learning, Steve requested a sommelier to guide him and his friends through a tasting. Hiring an expert doesn't need to be expensive—there are many young wine experts working their way up in the restaurant industry. The sommelier we chose encouraged conversation about the various types of BOND wines and answered any and all questions, so everyone left the table a little wiser.

OPPOSITE: We hired a sommelier to enlighten the men about BOND wines, shown here. FOLLOWING PAGES: Sleek gold and silver create a classic backdrop for a gentlemen's dinner.

OPPOSITE: Flickering votive-height candles make wineglasses appear to glow from within. THIS PAGE: When I planned this evening for my husband and his friends, I opted for masculine deep purple flowers, including the purple hellebores shown here in my grandmother's antique silver tureen.

BEET AND RED GREENS SALAD TOPPED WITH SAINT AGUR BLUE CHEESE

Saint Agur blue cheese from the Auvergne region of France pairs nicely with Steve's wine selection. The beets can be roasted a few days ahead and stored in the refrigerator.
Serves 6

2 bunches mixed color baby beets, trimmed
2 teaspoons vegetable oil
¼ cup thinly sliced red onion rings
3 tablespoons toasted walnut oil
2 tablespoons red wine vinegar
Salt and freshly ground black pepper to taste
8 cups loosely packed greens, such as lolla rossa,
   red Belgian endive, radicchio, butter lettuce,
   and baby beet greens
4 ounces blue cheese, crumbled
½ cup walnuts, toasted

Preheat the oven to 375°F. Arrange the beets in the center of a sheet of foil. Drizzle the beets with the vegetable oil and enclose in the foil. Roast the beets in the oven until tender, about 1 hour. Cool. (Can be prepared 3 days ahead; refrigerate.) Peel and slice the beets.

Whisk the shallot, walnut oil, and vinegar in a small bowl. Season the dressing to taste with salt and pepper.

Toss the beets with half of the dressing in a small bowl. Toss the greens with remaining dressing in a large shallow bowl. Divide the salad greens among 6 individual plates. Divide beets among the greens and sprinkle with walnuts and blue cheese and serve.

OPPOSITE AND LEFT: Decanting wine before serving is a must. Served in Moroccan tumblers with garlic aioli and ketchup, pommes frites become transcendent.

PREVIOUS PAGES: A fresh salad topped with deep-hued beets and Saint Agur blue cheese from the Auvergne region of France becomes unforgettable at the right place setting. THIS PAGE, CLOCKWISE FROM LEFT: Even butter gets an upgrade—with truffles and herbs. Roasted on a salt block, dry-aged porterhouse steak retains its juices. A variety of mushrooms such as enokitake, shimeji, and black trumpets add weighty depth to dishes. OPPOSITE: Rosemary and onions are a timeless accompaniment to a dry-aged porterhouse.

Cuttings of amaranthus in an Aerin vase echo the evening's free-flowing wine from BOND. After dinner, when more cigars are lit and whiskey begins to flow, it's time to arrange desserts, including gilt truffles and black and tan sundaes with homemade hot fudge and caramel sauces, on the sideboard.

OPPOSITE: Keep quick
nibbles within easy reach.
THIS PAGE: Stock a sideboard
with bar accoutrements
so they're always on hand.

CHOCOLATE FUDGE SAUCE

Makes about 1 ⅓ cups

½ cup firmly packed light brown sugar
2 tablespoons cocoa powder
¼ cup water
½ cup whipping cream
4 ounces bittersweet chocolate, chopped
½ teaspoon vanilla extract
¼ teaspoon salt

Whisk brown sugar and cocoa powder to blend in a heavy medium saucepan. Stir in water until smooth, then stir in the cream. Bring mixture to a simmer over medium heat, whisking occasionally to dissolve sugar. Let the mixture come to a boil. Remove from the heat and add the chocolate. Let stand until the chocolate melts. Add the vanilla and salt and whisk until smooth. (Can be prepared up to 1 week ahead. Cool, cover, and refrigerate. Rewarm, stirring, over medium heat.)

CARAMEL SAUCE

Makes about 1 ¼ cups

¾ cup sugar
¼ cup water
¾ cup whipping cream
2 tablespoons unsalted butter
Pinch of salt

Stir the sugar and water in heavy medium saucepan (preferably with a light-colored interior) over medium-low heat until the sugar dissolves. Increase the heat to medium and bring to a boil, without stirring. Brush down any crystals that form on the edge of the pan with a water-moistened pastry brush and cook until the mixture is a deep amber color, about 12 minutes. Remove from the heat and immediately pour in the cream (the mixture will bubble up) and whisk to blend. Add the butter and salt and stir until smooth. (Can be prepared up to 1 week ahead. Cool, cover, and refrigerate. Rewarm, stirring, over medium heat.)

BLACK AND TAN SUNDAES

Black and tan refers to chocolate and caramel sauces, respectively, in this soda fountain–style sundae.
Serves 6

1 batch Chocolate Fudge Sauce, warm
Toasted almond or vanilla ice cream
1 batch Caramel Sauce, warm
Toasted sliced almonds for garnish

Spoon a small amount (1 to 2 tablespoons) warm chocolate fudge sauce into a sundae glass. Top with a scoop of ice cream, then spoon some warm caramel sauce over the ice cream. Top with a second scoop of ice cream, then spoon over some chocolate sauce. Sprinkle with sliced almonds and serve.

ABOVE: Fresh blackberries add a pop of pinot-hued color to a sundae. OPPOSITE: Arranging bite-sized desserts on a three-tiered tray elevates their theatricality.

THIS PAGE: A caramel and nut tart is a rich, addictive late-night bite. OPPOSITE: Sugar cookies in playing card suits—spades, clubs, diamonds, and hearts—recall the fun of an old-fashioned poker night.

Group his favorite whiskeys together on a silver bar tray. Not only are they handy that way, but they're a conversation starter. Same goes for the cigars, laid out with all necessary regalia.

"I have a social disease. I have to go out every night. If I stay home one night I start spreading rumors to my dogs." —Andy Warhol

PERFECT PAIRINGS

DETERMINING WHAT WINES TO SERVE at your party with dinner is rarely easy. Consider seeking advice from an expert sommelier or your local wine store.

FOR A DINNER LIKE THIS, be sure to tailor the menu to wine. For example, a chilled Beaujolais Cru Gamay can highlight your pommes frites, and a cabernet is ideal for pairing with a dry-aged steak.

AS A CALIFORNIA GIRL, I gravitate toward California chardonnays. Two of my preferred vintners are Rombauer and Kistler.

FOR A MEN'S DINNER like this one, set up an after-dinner bar with cigars, special cocktail napkins, and beautiful crystal glasses ready to hold your husband's favorite whiskey.

A FAVORITE LONG-STANDING TRADITION OF MY HUSBAND'S is to have a whiskey and a cigar with a few of the men after dinner in a corner by the fireplace, the perfect spot for more intimate conversation. His go-to whiskey is Hibiki, from Japan.

When the playing cards come out, so do the edible versions.

Pucci by the Pool

y husband and I have a large blended family; between us we have seven children, most of them grown and living on their own. Our kids are an enormous part of our lives, so we look for moments to enjoy quality time together. Last August I plotted an afternoon pool and pizza party for our daughters and friends for a bit of unbridled fun.

In addition to pizza and pool, I found my inspiration in another hallowed P-word: Pucci. My obsession with Pucci—an Italian brand founded by Florentine noble Emilio Pucci in 1947, and famous for its undulating Technicolor prints—began two decades ago when I purchased a Pucci cover-up while on vacation at a beach resort in Italy. Pucci is instant chic, its prints every bit as fun and glamorous today as they were in 1972, when Grace Kelly lit up Palm Beach with her sherbet-hued Pucci top and candy-pink turban.

PARTY INSPIRATION:
PUCCI

PALETTE:
ORANGE, PURPLE, RASPBERRY,
AND MOSS GREEN

FLOWERS:
MULTIPLE TAFFY-PINK DAHLIAS IN LOW MILK
GLASS VASES AT EACH PLACE SETTING

TABLETOP ELEMENTS:
CHEERFUL PINK PLACEMATS AND
PINK AND ORANGE NAPKINS; IKAT PLATTERS;
RATTAN-WRAPPED WATER GLASSES

FOOD & DRINK:
SUMMERTIME PICNIC FARE
AND WOOD-FIRED PIZZA

———————

The energetic colors of Pucci's prints make a joyful palette for a party, an ideal match for the sunny hues of a Southern California afternoon. I brought Pucci's colors into the tablescape with placemats and napkins from Talmaris in Paris, my favorite tabletop store in the world, mixed with glasses from Crate & Barrel that I wouldn't fret about breaking. I dotted pink dahlias across our white picnic table to bring the garden forward. To create a special atmosphere tailored to your event, go custom on a few items. For this garden pool party, I had pool balls made out of a Pucci-inspired fabric that I had found while shopping; they kicked off an exuberant, playful mood.

I arranged multiple inviting seating areas around our garden so our guests would find plenty of room to stretch out and relax: chaise lounges under shady umbrellas abutting the pool (set with monogrammed towels, for a highly personal touch), a picnic table, and chairs set up on the lawn for tête-à-têtes for two. Because this was a casual affair, we didn't organize a party timeline, instead opting to keep things laid-back and free-form—guests could frolic in the pool or play spirited rounds of croquet at their leisure.

For the menu, I planned make-your-own pizzas that we would bake in the wood-fired outdoor pizza oven, plus platters of summer salads—like rainbow slaw and prosciutto with figs, melon, and mint. I also set out chevron-patterned bags of my custom party mix (truffle potato chips, popcorn, and pretzels) for easy snacking. To drink, we offered sodas in old-fashioned glass bottles and watermelon and orange ice refreshers with Aperol and Campari optional for the adults. There was only one hiccup: a bottle of rosé had turned—a nice reminder to check your wines before everyone has a pour!

Oranges from my family's Booth Ranches were used to serve summer cocktails, poolside icy drinks, and sorbet, adding some vibrant color with a California twist. Citrus is a natural representative of California—and just as bright, fresh, and delicious as Pucci itself.

OPPOSITE: Arranging multiple shaded seating areas—pool chaises, picnic tables, and benches—allows your guests to flit around the grounds like butterflies. FOLLOWING PAGES: My passion for Pucci sparked this exuberant afternoon, complete with custom beach balls in a vintage Pucci-inspired print.

THESE AND FOLLOWING PAGES: When you host a party in a lush garden, you can go wild with color. Red, orange, turquoise, lavender—everything coordinates with green. Even the straws in a chevron pattern and rainbow hues get into the spirit of summer fun.

OPPOSITE: The vivid hues of citrus fruits join in riotous splendor on the tablescape and make the other colors—rouge pink, avocado green— all the more luscious. THIS PAGE: Italian glasses filled with watermelon and orange ice refreshers (Aperol and Campari optional).

Successful pool time requires snacks. All ages can appreciate ready-to-go nibbles, like my custom party mix (pretzels, truffle potato chips, and popcorn) in paper chevron treat bags. Lemonade and orange soda in beautiful glass bottles evoke a picnic spirit.

THIS PAGE: Mixing textures and colors on a tabletop creates a warm, carefree feeling that puts people at ease. OPPOSITE: Pink dahlias simply placed in colorful water glasses are so happy-looking, a kind of floral firework, ideal for welcoming guests to an al fresco luncheon.

PREVIOUS PAGES: Plentiful platters of summer salads—such as a rainbow slaw and prosciutto with figs, melon, and mint—summon the feeling of a picnic on the Amalfi Coast. OPPOSITE: A graphic ikat plate sets an eye-catching stage. THIS PAGE, CLOCKWISE FROM LEFT: Teddy stands watch over a crate of citrus from our family groves, Booth Ranches. Fragrant oranges embody California freshness more than anything else. Our youngest King Charles cavalier, Emma, is ready to play ball with the guests.

Who doesn't love pizza? We invited guests to top their own pies with fresh mozzarella and other Italian cheeses, garden tomatoes, shrimp, prosciutto, arugula, and herbs, then baked them in our outdoor wood-burning oven. OPPOSITE: Monogrammed custom pizza boxes let guests bring any leftover bites home in a memorable way.

WATERMELON AND ORANGE
ICE REFRESHERS; ROSÉ; LEMONADE
AND ORANGE SODA

WOOD-FIRED-OVEN PIZZAS

SUMMER SALADS
(RAINBOW SLAW; PROSCIUTTO
WITH FIGS, MELON, AND MINT)

PARTY MIX WITH PRETZELS,
TRUFFLE POTATO CHIPS, AND POPCORN

SORBET IN FROZEN
HOLLOWED ORANGE PEELS

———————

WATERMELON AND ORANGE ICE REFRESHERS

These are a fun take on snow cones. Adults can "spike" their refreshers with chilled vodka, if desired.
Makes about 12 drinks

5 cups fresh watermelon cubes
⅓ cup freshly squeezed lime juice
¼ cup plus 2 tablespoons sugar
2 tablespoons Campari (optional)
4 cups freshly squeezed orange juice
2 tablespoons freshly squeezed lemon juice
1 dash orange flower water
2 tablespoons Aperol (optional)

Combine the watermelon, lime juice, and ¼ cup sugar in a blender and puree until smooth. Strain the watermelon mixture into a large measuring cup and add Campari, if using. In another large measuring cup, combine the orange juice, lemon juice, remaining 2 tablespoons sugar, and orange flower water and stir until the sugar dissolves. Stir in Aperol, if using. Pour the watermelon and orange mixtures into ice cube trays and freeze.

Just before serving, crush the frozen cubes in a blender until slushy. Divide among small glasses and serve.

PIZZA WITH CHERRY TOMATOES, GOAT CHEESE, AND FRESH HERB DRIZZLE

We're lucky to have a wood-burning oven by our pool where we cook pizzas, but this recipe has been adapted for use in an indoor oven. There will be enough herb mixture to enjoy on three to four pizzas. Leftovers are delicious as a topping on almost anything—toasted bread, pasta, stirred into some hummus. Pick up fresh dough at your favorite pizzeria.
Makes one 12-inch pizza, about 6 servings

½ cup minced fresh basil leaves
¼ cup minced flat-leaf parsley leaves
2 tablespoons minced fresh oregano leaves
⅓ cup extra-virgin olive oil, plus more for brushing
Semolina flour for sprinkling
8 ounces fresh pizza dough
1 garlic clove, crushed with a garlic press
1 ½ cups (about 6 ounces) grated mozzarella cheese
1 cup very small cherry tomatoes, halved
Salt and freshly ground black pepper
3 ounces crumbled goat cheese

Position one rack in the top third of the oven and one rack in the bottom third and preheat the oven to 400°F. Stir the basil, parsley, oregano and ⅓ cup olive oil to blend in a small bowl. Sprinkle a large heavy baking sheet lightly with semolina flour (about 1 tablespoon). Roll the dough out on a lightly floured surface to a 12-inch round. Transfer the dough to the prepared baking sheet and brush with oil. Using your fingertips or the back of a spoon, spread the garlic over the pizza. Sprinkle evenly with the mozzarella. Top with the tomatoes. Season the pizza lightly with salt and generously with pepper and sprinkle on the goat cheese. Bake on the bottom rack until the bottom of the pizza is golden brown, about 15 minutes. Transfer to the top rack and bake until the top is golden, about 3 additional minutes. Transfer the pizza to a cutting board and drizzle on some of the herb mixture. Cut into wedges and serve.

Using hollowed frozen oranges as serving vessels not only means dessert can be made ahead, but also that the fruit and berry sorbets will stay frozen longer in the warm afternoon air.

"Color is my day-long obsession, joy, and torment." — Claude Monet

CONSIDERATIONS FOR BRILLIANT PARTIES AL FRESCO

HOSTING A PARTY OUTDOORS allows you more freedom with your color palette. Working with the lush green of a garden or the bright turquoise of a pool gives you a chance to experiment with bright, colorful hues without fretting about matching your house's décor.

COORDINATE GROUP ACTIVITIES, such as croquet and other games, to get guests moving and mingling.

IT CAN BE FUN TO CREATE custom take-home containers for leftovers. We monogrammed pizza boxes, which allowed guests to bring nibbles home with them easily. It's easy enough to take a plain pizza box and make it special with monogrammed stickers ordered online from sites like Etsy or Zazzle or printed at home on Avery labels.

ARRANGE A BASKET OF POOL-PARTY NECESSITIES: sunscreen, lip balm with SPF, flip-flops, extra bathing suits, fluffy towels, hats, and any toiletries that guests might need.

When planning these custom beach balls, I selected a Pucci-inspired print that would play well with the turquoise hues of our pool.

Dinner Under the Stars

I have always been captivated by astrology and horoscopes, because I believe there is so much more to life than meets the eye. So when I treated myself to a series of celestial china by Milanese ceramicist Costanza Paravicini, I felt—well—the stars aligning. I decided to use the plates, which render the zodiac in exquisite, saturated hues and glimmering gold constellations, as my muse for a couples' dinner in our garden loggia.

Couples' dinner parties are among my favorite ways to entertain, because you can catch up with multiple friends at once in one lovely night. I prefer to invite an unexpected mix, so that not everyone knows one another—a surefire path to sparkling conversation and new friendships formed.

PARTY INSPIRATION:
ASTROLOGY AND CELESTIAL CHINA
BY COSTANZA PARAVICINI

PALETTE:
DARK CHOCOLATE, GOLD,
AND CERULEAN BLUE

FLOWERS:
PINK AND LIME HYDRANGEAS,
APRICOT CARPE DIEM ROSES, BROWN SWEET
PEAS, AND CAPPUCCINO BEIGE ROSES

TABLETOP ELEMENTS:
STAR SIGN SCROLLS AT EACH SEAT;
CHOCOLATE VELVET TABLECLOTHS;
STAR AND MOON GOLD-EMBROIDERED
DINNER AND COCKTAIL NAPKINS;
BLACK TAPER CANDLES; AMBER VOTIVES

FOOD & DRINK:
A GREEK FEAST

Our loggia had been designed as a de facto outdoor living room, complete with heaters tucked away in the ceiling to keep everyone comfortable during the cooler dusk hours. That evening, we replaced the sofas with a pair of long tables that would seat a total of twenty-six guests by the flickering glow of the fire, with me at the head of one and Steve at the other.

Planning a few unexpected surprises for your guests leads to the most memorable nights. Building on our zodiac theme, I hired a beloved Los Angeles psychic to perch herself in the living room during cocktail hour, proffering her visions to whoever wanted to sit with her. It was a hit! Even some of the most skeptical men in attendance got a kick out of it. I also topped each place setting with a golden scroll tied with a satin ribbon and a charm representing the star sign of that guest. (I'd asked them for their zodiac signs on the RSVP card.) Once unfurled, each scroll laid out the hallmarks of that guest's particular personality traits.

For the menu, I let the zodiac point me to Greece. Steve and I make an annual trip there every summer to unwind and rejuvenate, soaking up the rhythm, the fresh, unfussy meals that linger into the night, and that omnipresent sun. The menu I chose nodded to all of that, from abundant tasting platters of grape leaf dolmas, hummus, and olive tapenade, to a buffet of grilled wild salmon fillets and lamb skewers that had been marinated in Greek yogurt and lemon, to the ouzo bar and palate-cleansing dessert: Greek yogurt topped with homemade hemp seed granola, local honey, sea salt, and Greek olive oil. Our specialty cocktail for the night—a relaxing lavender-infused vodka drink—said "let your hair down" with each sip.

For the tables, I selected rich, chocolate velvet cloths to ground the vivid zodiac plates and let the apricot and Mediterranean blue hues within them shine. I set out star and moon cocktail and dinner napkins and a smattering of amber votives to twinkle across the tabletop celestially. Bursting flower arrangements—of dusky brown sweet peas, cappuccino beige roses, variegated pink hydrangeas, and Carpe Diem apricot roses—lent a layer of abundant softness to the spread that anyone, no matter their astrological sign, could admire.

OPPOSITE: For this celestial dinner party on our loggia, I selected flowers in saturated hues to supply poetic beauty atop chocolate velvet table linens. FOLLOWING PAGES: Everyone enjoys dinner by candlelight.

THIS PAGE, CLOCKWISE FROM TOP LEFT: Place cards with embossed gold dots evoke bubbling Champagne. It was the perfect evening to break out my star and moon gold embroidered dinner napkins. Delicate sweet peas emit a divine, subtle scent. OPPOSITE: Purple and green hydrangeas have a mystical aura. FOLLOWING PAGES: I found my muse in zodiac china by Milanese ceramicist Costanza Paravicini and ran with it, placing a custom horoscope scroll for each guest at their place setting.

THE MENU

VODKA LEMON KISS COCKTAILS GARNISHED
WITH SPRIGS OF LAVENDER AND
LEMON TWISTS; OUZO BAR;
TENUTA SAN GUIDO GUIDALBERTO AND
JERMANN PINOT GRIGIO WINE

LAMB SKEWERS WITH YOGURT SAUCE

GRILLED WILD SALMON FILLET

CAULIFLOWER RICE TABBOULEH

DOLMAS, HUMMUS, AND OLIVE TAPENADE

GREEK SALAD

GREEK YOGURT TOPPED WITH
HEMP SEED GRANOLA, LOCAL HONEY,
SEA SALT, AND OLIVE OIL

PISTACHIO BAKLAVA DRIZZLED WITH HONEY

———————————

LAMB KEBABS WITH YOGURT AND CUCUMBER SAUCE

The yogurt sauce, or tzatziki, can be made up to 3 days ahead and refrigerated.
Serves 6

YOGURT SAUCE
1 cup Greek yogurt or ²/₃ cup plain yogurt
    and ¹/₃ cup sour cream
1 small garlic clove, crushed with a garlic press
2 Persian cucumbers, quartered and sliced,
    or 1 standard cucumber, peeled, quartered,
    seeded, and sliced
1 green onion, sliced
2 tablespoons minced fresh dill
Salt and freshly ground black pepper to taste

LAMB
3 tablespoons extra-virgin olive oil, plus more for brushing
3 garlic cloves, crushed with a garlic press
1 teaspoon ground cumin
1 teaspoon kosher salt
1 teaspoon dried marjoram
1 teaspoon dried mint
1 teaspoon paprika
¹/₂ teaspoon freshly ground black pepper
2 pounds boneless leg of lamb, cut into 1 ¹/₂-inch cubes

For the sauce, in a medium bowl, blend the yogurt and garlic. Add the cucumbers, green onion, and dill. Season the sauce lightly with salt and generously with pepper; mix well.

For the lamb, in a large bowl, combine the 3 tablespoons olive oil and all the other ingredients except the meat and whisk to blend. Add the lamb and toss to coat with the garlic mixture. Cover and let the lamb stand 20 minutes at room temperature or overnight in the refrigerator.

Prepare a grill to medium-high heat. Thread the lamb onto metal skewers, dividing evenly. Brush the kebabs with olive oil. Grill, turning occasionally, about 7 to 9 minutes for medium-rare. Transfer to plates and serve with the yogurt sauce.

PREVIOUS PAGE: A Greek and Mediterranean menu—including lamb kebabs with yogurt sauce—was the only way to go, given the celestial theme. RIGHT: Arranging a self-serve ouzo bar on one side of the loggia inspires guests to mix and mingle.

Shot glasses with gilt Greek key detailing make imbibing
ouzo a ceremony. OPPOSITE, CLOCKWISE FROM TOP LEFT:
Silvery mint julep cups are the ideal size for bar snacks,
such as vegetable chips. The evening's tart vodka lemon
kiss cocktail, garnished with a sprig of lavender and
fragrant lemon peel. V-shaped glasses subtly colored in
garnet, peach, seafoam, and smoke catch the light.

LEMON KISS COCKTAIL

For large parties, make a big batch of the base for this light, tart drink to pour over crushed ice as guests arrive.

Makes 12 drinks

1 ½ cups vodka
¾ cup freshly squeezed lemon juice
½ cup limoncello liqueur
14 sprigs fresh lavender
12 ¾ x 3-inch strips fresh lemon peel
Crushed ice

Stir vodka, lemon juice, and limoncello together in a large pitcher. Add 2 sprigs of the lavender and refrigerate until chilled. (You can to do this the day before and refrigerate overnight.)

Roll each lemon peel strip around a lavender sprig and secure with a cocktail pick. Fill 12 coupe glasses with crushed ice. Remove the lavender sprigs from the vodka mixture and stir to blend. Pour over ice, garnish with prepared lemon peel and lavender, and serve.

PREVIOUS PAGES: Rich sapphire blue velvet tablecloths turn peachy pink garden roses into the stars of an already starry evening.

RIGHT: Ample dishes of classic Greek desserts— such as halvah, dates, and kataifi—allow guests to sample a bit of everything.

THIS PAGE, CLOCKWISE FROM TOP LEFT: Guests go wild for thoughtful little touches, like these glimmering matchboxes emblazoned with star signs. Starry, gold-rimmed plates and monogrammed cocktail napkins add pomp to cocktail hour. I tied each guest's scroll with a charm featuring their specific star sign. OPPOSITE: Bursting cherry branches draw the eye skyward.

"I have learned that to be with those I like is enough." —Walt Whitman

A COUPLES' SOIRÉE

WHEN YOU'RE PLANNING THE SEATING arrangement for a couples dinner party, mix it up! Sometimes I'll seat couples at opposite corners of the same table, or even place them at different tables altogether. Although wallflowers might balk, it's much more fun for the two halves of a pair who are always together to have distinct experiences and then share them on the way home. I've also found that more new friendships are born this way.

AN EASY PLOY TO SPUR CONVERSATION with couples is to put an icebreaker right on the table, such as the zodiac scrolls I created for this starry evening. Make it something unexpected enough to be exciting and it will spark dialogue that's much more interesting than the latest weather report!

PREVENT HUNGER BEFORE DINNER by keeping nibbles at the bar that guests can snack on while they're ordering drinks.

SETTING OUT A BUFFET for the main course forces your guests to get up and mingle. There is an art to a buffet, though: I like to keep food at room temperature so no one has to endure a cold dinner and guests can easily go back for more.

I PREFER BUFFET PLATES over dinner plates. They're larger—often twelve inches or more across—and can hold more food graciously. Abundance is one of my personal mottos!

KEEP BACKGROUND MUSIC ON from the moment guests arrive to the second they depart, so there's never a lull in the evening.

SERVE A LIGHT, fresh dessert to cleanse the palate. In case any of my guests have big sweet tooths, I'll also prepare a cookie plate to pass around.

FOR THE DESSERT COURSE, I'll often encourage guests to move over a few spaces and meet someone new. Sometimes it doesn't work because they end up sitting next to their spouse, and at that point I just throw up my hands and laugh. You can sit wherever you like, as long as you're enjoying the conversation!

Like stars twinkling in the night sky, my celestial china pops against a dark chocolate velvet tablecloth.

Holiday Magic

Christmas comes at an ideal time of year—when days are short, a chill is in the air, and it is even more important to spend time with loved ones. I always adore the season and have so many fond memories of Christmas from my childhood, because my mom made each Christmas very special. Once I had my own family, I continued some of her traditions and added new ones of my own, all with the goal of bringing the same sense of delight to Christmas.

I grew up opening my stocking in my parents' bedroom while they sipped their morning coffee. My mom always hid one present that we would get to open before breakfast. When I was 12, all I wanted was a pair of white roller skates with red wheels, and I found them lined up in her shoe closet alongside her heels! When my own children were younger, I incorporated the tradition of hiding surprise gifts. (One year, I even hid a hamster!)

PARTY INSPIRATION:
CHRISTMAS CHEER

PALETTE:
RED, WHITE, EVERGREEN, SLEIGH-BELL
SILVER, AND POWDER BLUE

FLOWERS:
WHITE AND RED AMARYLLIS, PAPERWHITES,
RANUNCULUS, AND PEONIES

TABLETOP ELEMENTS:
GLIMMERING GOLD AND SILVER BLOWN
GLASS ORNAMENTS; TEDDY BEAR MOSS
TOPIARIES HOLDING SILVER-WRAPPED
GIFTS TRIMMED IN GREEN VELVET
RIBBON; GRAY NAPKINS; AND GIFTS
ADORNED WITH EVERGREEN SPRIGS AND
GREEN RIBBON AT EACH PLACE

FOOD & DRINK:
A HEARTY BRUNCH

It's even more impactful to create your own holiday traditions that are authentic and unique to your own family and inspired by your own passions. These days, when I am creating Christmas at home—whether we're celebrating in Los Angeles or Sun Valley, Idaho—I still like to thrill my children. I plan experiences for us to share together, each of which can be tailored to your own family. We typically wake up to don new matching pajamas, open our stockings, and eat a big decadent breakfast (like eggs benedict, fresh fruit salad, and bacon-sausage scones). Then we have a long, leisurely day of opening presents and enjoying one another's company. I put up a buffet on the sideboard in the living room with a Bloody Mary bar for our adult children and easy-to-eat nibbles, like a variety of mini brioche sandwiches and crisp potato chips.

Some family members might take a break from holiday prep by going snowshoeing or skiing (or indulging in a nap) before we all go out for dinner.

To bring the Christmas spirit into your home in a way that lasts the entire season, keep the refrigerator and bar well-stocked (hot chocolate is a must), have merry holiday music playing in the background, and have scented candles on hand. You'll want to dress the house in tons of herbaceous decorations; this year, I selected a dreamy palette of soft blues, Santa reds, and silver that gleamed like icicles and topped each table with ample boughs of cut evergreen and white seasonal flowers (paperwhites, white amaryllis, and peonies). Because two of my passions are my King Charles cavaliers and topiaries, I sourced gift wrap that depicted both in watercolor renderings. The world is at your fingertips these days—just punch in your passion and you'll likely find exactly what you are seeking online. My three dogs, Emma, Oliver, and Teddy, even had special collars and personalized dishes for the holiday and, of course, their own stockings and tree, too. I could swear it gave them an added twinkle in their eyes.

OPPOSITE: A native of South Africa, amaryllis is beloved in the winter months for its ability to bloom indoors.
FOLLOWING PAGES: It's the little details, like these customized stockings, that they'll remember for years to come.

Even in Los Angeles, fresh blossoms usher in a dose of springtime necessary in the dead of winter. OPPOSITE: This time of year, white flowers evoke Jack Frost's dusting of snow. THIS PAGE, CLOCKWISE FROM LEFT: Paperwhites, white amaryllis, and peonies.

SPICED BLOODY MARYS

We like to serve Bloody Marys on Christmas morning with an assortment of fun garnishes: skewers of olives and onions, Italian peppers, celery and fennel sticks, green onions, and even pretzel rods.
Makes 10 drinks

6 cups best-quality tomato juice, chilled
3 cups vodka
⅔ cup freshly squeezed lemon juice
1 tablespoon hot sauce, such as Tabasco
1 tablespoon Worcestershire sauce
1 teaspoon freshly grated lemon zest
1 teaspoon smoked paprika
1 teaspoon celery salt
Freshly ground white pepper to taste

Stir the tomato juice, vodka, lemon juice, hot sauce, Worcestershire sauce, lemon zest, paprika, and celery salt in a large pitcher. Add pepper to taste. Pour over ice and have guests garnish as desired.

CLASSIC CHRISTMAS COOKIES

In our family we decorate these tender, crisp cookies with colored sugar, royal icing, and sprinkles. The cookies make great hostess gifts.
Makes about 4 dozen cookies

2 ½ cups unbleached all-purpose flour
1 teaspoon baking powder
½ teaspoon salt
1 cup (2 sticks) unsalted butter, at room temperature
¾ cup sugar
1 large egg
1 teaspoon vanilla extract

In a medium bowl, whisk the flour, baking powder, and salt to blend. Using an electric mixer, cream the butter and sugar in a large bowl until very light and fluffy. Beat in the egg and vanilla extract. Gradually blend in the flour mixture.

Divide the dough into 4 equal portions. Shape each portion of dough into a ball, then flatten them into disks. Wrap each dough disk in plastic wrap and chill until firm, about 4 hours minimum. (The dough can be made up to 4 days ahead. Keep refrigerated.)

Preheat the oven to 350°F. Line large heavy baking sheets with parchment paper. On a lightly floured work surface, roll out a dough disk ¼ inch thick. Using cookie cutters, cut out desired shapes. Transfer the cutouts to the prepared baking sheets. Gather and reroll scraps. Repeat with the remaining dough disks.

Bake the cookies in batches until golden on the edges, about 10 minutes. Transfer the cookies to racks to cool. Cool completely before decorating.

On Christmas day, I arrange a buffet of mini brioche sandwiches and chips, so we have sustenance for the fun hours ahead. A spicy Bloody Mary bar with unexpected garnishes—fennel sticks, pretzel rods, and skewered olives—keeps the adults in a jolly mood worthy of Santa himself.

Is there anything that creates more family fun than decorating cookies together? Maximize the moment with only-at-Christmas toppings, such as decorettes, edible gold and silver sugar pearls, gold paint for monogramming, and candied citrus.

No matter how far they roam or how much they're grown, they're still our children on Christmas morning—and we love outfitting them in matching pajamas. This cuteness comes but once a year! This time, we opted for white-piped flannel PJs in Santa-suit red and embroidered each pair with the wearer's monogram for a personal touch. ABOVE: Izzi, Ande, Charlotte, and Harrison pre-gaming their presents. LEFT: My son Harrison holding Emma, our youngest and a gift to me from my husband. OPPOSITE: The personalized pajamas and ornaments were set by the chimney with care . . . FOLLOWING PAGES: Our over-the-top breakfast on Christmas morning includes a buffet for easy grazing—with an eye-catching herd of metallic forest fauna.

OPPOSITE: Cranberry and raspberry yogurt parfaits conjure snowcapped peaks. THIS PAGE, CLOCKWISE FROM LEFT: Garnish hot chocolate as prettily as you would a cocktail for an all-ages delight. Ginger, cranberry, and currant scones are among the sumptuous treats that help make the season special. On the breakfast table, a centerpiece of verdant greens evokes the spirit of the winter woods. FOLLOWING PAGES: Fragrant paperwhites—a favorite for the holidays—take center stage at the breakfast table, where teddy bear moss topiaries add to the fun.

OPPOSITE: Placing a gift at each seat will put a smile on their faces before they've even had their coffee. THIS PAGE: Custom embroidered linen napkins offer the warmest possible welcome to the table: if they're in a timeless gray hue you'll use them all year long.

Charlotte

OPPOSITE: On a sideboard, our dogs have their own area, complete with an out-of-reach tree.

THIS PAGE, CLOCKWISE FROM TOP LEFT: Customized gift wrap and stationery tailored to your passions, such as my topiary meets King Charles cavalier pattern, is the ultimate personal touch. In our house, even the dogs receive gifts. Dog bowls emblazoned with their names—and dancing Santas—are a whimsical seasonal treat.

> *"Where we love is home—home that our feet may leave, but not our hearts."*
> — Oliver Wendell Holmes, Sr.

FAMILY CHRISTMAS: TOGETHERNESS TIPS

THE MONTH OF DECEMBER is often a revolving door for me, so I decorate early—the day after Thanksgiving. The earlier, the merrier.

WHEN THE HOLIDAYS DESCEND, be prepared to welcome your children and their spouses, cousins, friends, grandparents, and anyone else who might cross your threshold. Always have a full fridge so you can pull together nibbles and assorted beverages for anyone who might drop by.

IT'S NEVER TOO LATE to start new family traditions. One of the longstanding traditions in our house is that everyone gets matching fun pajamas every year. We've all donned PJs in prints from leopard to candy canes. This year, we did custom monogrammed ones in red flannel with white trim, a classic touch.

PLAN ONE OR TWO SEASONAL TRADITIONS in which guests can opt to participate if they like, such as cookie decorating or a secret Santa gift exchange.

HERE'S A FUN GIFT IDEA: Personalize a gingerbread house with your friends' or family members' names written on the rooftop in frosting.

EVERYONE SHOULD HAVE a stocking with his or her name on it, even pets!

MAKE TIME TO CELEBRATE with your spouse, too, in private. Steve and I wake up a little early Christmas morning to sip coffee and exchange gifts.

I OFTEN PUT SOMETHING ON THE STOVE to fill the house with the spirit and scent of the season, such as mulled cider. It smells just like Christmas.

IF YOU HAVE HOUSEGUESTS, be sure to leave fresh flowers in their rooms, along with an abundance of towels, new toiletries, and good books by their bedsides.

Early on Christmas morning, Steve and I share a moment together in our master suite. We exchange gifts over cups of tea and freshly baked scones before joining our large blended family for a day of cheer. Blue and white is one of my go-to seasonal color palettes. It evokes the clear skies and fresh powder of the slopes in Sun Valley, Idaho.

A Chic Dinner
in the City

Some things never go out of style. Champagne, caviar, martinis, smoked salmon—they're simple and sophisticated and they always wow. For this wintertime cocktail and dinner party at our New York City apartment on the Upper East Side—in a thirty-eight-story tower designed by Schultze & Weaver in 1927—that overlooks Central Park, I let classic New York serve as my inspiration. Manhattan is among the most forward-thinking twenty-two square miles on the planet, and it is archetypal in every way. Everything, from the Beaux-Arts architecture of The Metropolitan Museum of Art to the 1914 neoclassical Frick Collection, conjures a cinematic version of the city that will live on forever.

PARTY INSPIRATION:
CLASSIC NEW YORK

PALETTE:
BLACK AND WHITE AND METALLICS

FLOWERS:
WHITE POM-POM DAHLIAS, WHITE HYBRID
DELPHINIUMS, BURGUNDY PEONIES,
AND WHITE GARDEN ROSES

TABLETOP ELEMENTS:
BLACK TAPER CANDLES; EBONY WATER
GLASSES; GILT NAPKIN RINGS; BLACK
AND WHITE LINENS

FOOD & DRINK:
CLASSIC MID-CENTURY COCKTAIL
PARTY FARE

To forge a city-chic vibe, I chose a black and white palette. It's a classic mix, yet it's not traditional or tired. I used tall black taper candles and ebony-hued water glasses to coordinate with the black and white Greek key trim on the tablecloths. Continuing the only-in-New York aesthetic, silver trays reflected the light and shimmered like the skyline outside the windows. For my flowers, I selected seasonal blooms—white pom-pom dahlias, hybrid delphiniums, and burgundy peonies—corralled into single color groups for dramatic impact and placed at varying heights for dimension. I also set white garden roses in the entry hall to make a welcoming, pretty statement guests would see the moment they walked in.

The menu featured abundant hors d'oeuvre, many of which turned comfort food into something truly indulgent, such as cheese toasts or deviled eggs topped with caviar. I prefer to serve foods that I enjoy eating. There is no point in entertaining to impress people—entertaining has to come from a generosity of spirit and things you authentically love yourself! At the same time, adding an extra twist like caviar makes guests feel pampered and spoiled, in the very best way. We also served seared scallops with endive salads and set out plentiful seafood towers with lobster, shrimp, oysters, crawfish, and crab, plus a caviar, blini, and vodka bar. Our drinks were upgraded classics, too: vodka martinis with rosemary swizzles; gin and tonics with ice embedded prettily with rose petals and lemon; and copious Champagne.

Starting a dinner party with a cocktail hour allows guests whose conflicting schedules won't allow them to stay for the full evening enjoy a bit of merriment. To help with flow in a small space, you can set up separate stations in different rooms to maximize the floor plan. Here I served drinks in the living room with lots of passed appetizers before we sat down to an intimate dinner in the dining room. It's vital to make the best use of your space, because you always want a room to feel full, so the energy of abundant laughter and conversation reigns over all.

That evening, one of my friends brought a guest we didn't know and who didn't know any of the other guests. I greeted her as she entered and we had a really nice conversation. At the end of the night, she came over and said, "You made me feel welcome and comfortable the minute I walked in the door; thank you for a wonderful evening!" It reminded me, as a hostess, how important it is to greet people. Every party I host is about sharing myself. When it happens to the sound of clinking Champagne glasses with new friends at my side, that's all the better.

THIS PAGE: There's nothing more welcoming than a bevy of blooms. FOLLOWING PAGES: My designer, Jeffrey Bilhuber, arranged an ideal space for entertaining in a limited footprint. Three seating areas allow guests to mix and mingle within easy reach of the bar.

I often gather flowers in a single color in graphic vases throughout my New York apartment; garden freshness is always appreciated in an urban environment.

In New York City, a classic black and white palette exudes the same glamour as tuxedoed gentlemen at The Met. Black taper candles call to mind Manhattan's soaring skyline. The custom banquette maximizes space.

PREVIOUS PAGES: Mixing metals and black and white crystal is a nod to the cityscape beyond the windows. OPPOSITE: I adore Greek key detailing and love the graphic accent it brings to this table. Keep bud vases low to allow conversation to flow. Eye contact is a must! THIS PAGE, CLOCKWISE FROM LEFT: Guests appreciate the tiniest of details—like their names exquisitely rendered in calligraphy on place cards. Appropriate accoutrements—caviar spoons made of mother of pearl; oyster forks— keep the proceedings feeling flawless. Gilt napkin rings make any tablescape sparkle.

THIS PAGE: Glorious shoots of hybrid delphiniums seem to burst from a faceted gilt vase and sparkle against a dark backdrop. OPPOSITE: Every detail tells the story of the evening—and each, in its way, is a mirror of Manhattan, all right angles and raucous splendor. FOLLOWING PAGES: A room-temperature buffet is a busy hostess's secret weapon: she can spend less time worrying about the food and more time kicking up her heels.

OPPOSITE: Oysters on the half shell are a fun finger food that also feels indulgent. THIS PAGE: Old-fashioned white toast points are transcendent with smoked salmon and a bevy of lobster, shrimp, and crab.

THIS PAGE: A tray of caviar and vodka shots is guaranteed to make guests' eyes pop with delight. OPPOSITE: Party favorites, like deviled eggs and herbed cream cheese–stuffed cucumbers, can be dressed up with a bit of caviar or salmon roe.

DEVILED EGGS WITH CHIVES AND CAVIAR

This simple approach to seasoning the eggs allows the caviar to star in a fancy take on a party favorite.
Makes 12 hors d'oeuvre

6 eggs
3 tablespoons sour cream
2 tablespoons mayonnaise
2 teaspoons Dijon mustard
1 tablespoon snipped fresh chives
Salt to taste
¼ cup caviar

Place the eggs in a small saucepan, add water to cover, and bring to a simmer. Simmer for 5 minutes. Remove the saucepan from the heat, cover, and let stand 5 minutes. Rinse the eggs under cold water. Refrigerate the eggs until chilled.

Peel and halve the eggs. Remove the yolks and transfer to a medium bowl. Mash the yolks with a fork. Mix in the sour cream, mayonnaise, and mustard until smooth. Fold in most of the chives and season with salt. Spoon the yolk mixture into the egg whites. Carefully spoon 1 teaspoon of caviar atop each egg, garnish with a piece or two of chive, and serve.

SEARED SCALLOPS WITH BUTTER LETTUCE AND ENDIVE

Searing in a hot skillet is the best way to cook scallops—the outsides get browned and finely crisped and the insides stay moist and sweet.
Serves 6

DRESSING
3 tablespoons freshly squeezed lemon juice
2 tablespoons minced shallot
2 teaspoons minced fresh tarragon
1 ½ teaspoons Dijon mustard
2 tablespoons extra-virgin olive oil
2 tablespoons grapeseed oil
Salt and freshly ground white pepper to taste

SALAD AND SCALLOPS
1 head butter lettuce, separated into leaves
2 heads endive, trimmed into spears
2 tablespoons grapeseed oil
18 jumbo scallops, about 1 pound
Salt and freshly ground white pepper to taste

For the dressing, in a small bowl whisk the lemon juice, shallot, tarragon, and mustard. Gradually whisk in the olive and grapeseed oils. Season to taste with salt and pepper.

For the salad, arrange the lettuce leaves and endive spears on 6 individual salad plates.

Heat the grapeseed oil in a large heavy skillet over high heat. Season the scallops with salt and pepper and add to the skillet. Sear, turning once, until the scallops are well browned on both sides but just barely cooked in the center, about 1 ½ minutes per side. Transfer the scallops to the salad plates, dividing evenly. Drizzle the dressing over the salads and serve.

An endive salad with seared scallops clears the palate for courses to come.

OPPOSITE: A tray of ready-made martinis announces that the party awaits. THIS PAGE, CLOCKWISE FROM LEFT: Even ice takes on an aura of opulence when embedded with lemon peel and rose petals, an ideal upgrade for a gin and tonic. Swizzles made from rosemary skewering olives and onions elevate the classic martini. Fruit-infused ice cubes add color and sparkle like gems in a Champagne digestif.

"Be pretty if you can, be witty if you must, but be gracious if it kills you." — Elsie de Wolfe

LUXURY IN A SMALL SPACE

IN AN INTIMATE SETTING, such as a New York pied-à-terre, it is vital to edit everything down to its essence in keeping with the theme for the night. Repetition (like the limited palette of black, white, burgundy, and metallic shown here) is key to keeping with the theme in a small space.

TO AVOID COOKING A LAVISH MEAL IN A CRAMPED KITCHEN, opt for easy edibles that impress: tiered trays of seafood, such as lobster and shrimp, or caviar, crème fraîche, and blinis, and bubbly Champagne!

FOR A COCKTAIL PARTY, select room-temperature foods, so that you don't have to be as worried about timing.

MY FAVORITE CLASSIC DRINKS are Veuve Clicquot Rosé Champagne or a good old-fashioned vodka martini, icy cold, with three olives, not two.

LIGHT CANDLES AN HOUR BEFORE guests arrive so a beautiful scent fills your home. I love Nest's bamboo-scented candle.

Check your tablescape one last time before guests arrive to ensure everything is in place. Light the candles, turn on your playlist—and then have a cocktail.

The Big Event:
A Fiftieth
Birthday Party

When I turned fifty, I longed to celebrate in our garden with all of our family and friends at my side. At the same time, I wanted to do something that would transport everyone, without requiring a destination weekend. Creating magic is possible for a large-scale event—you just need to find the right muse to cast a spell. For inspiration I chose one of my favorite vacation spots, Saint-Tropez—the storied town of about five thousand on the glimmering Côte d'Azur.

Bagatelle
Bel Air

Stephanie's 50th

Bagatelle

STEPHANIE'S 50th
BIRTHDAY WISH

So let me tell you a little secret
Which will be a secret no more
I don't want your presents,
Instead I want your presence for what's in store

This is a party for my dearest friends
And for a half-century occasion,
I want your smiling face on the dance floor
With no excuses or evasion!

So my wish is for you to stay,
For you to dance the night away,
Join me in a celebration of fun and friendship
That makes the word 50 easier to say!

PLEASE NO GIFTS
UBER RECOMMENDED

Greeting guests personally, with drinks on hand, is key to ensuring they feel at home instantly. By flanking our entry portico with images of Saint-Tropez—hung from hedges installed just for the occasion and strung with twinkling lights—we helped our friends feel transported the moment they stepped out of their cars.

PARTY INSPIRATION:
SAINT-TROPEZ AND THE RESTAURANTS
BAGATELLE AND LE BILBOQUET

PALETTE:
MEDITERRANEAN BLUE, CLOUD WHITE,
AND SILVER

FLOWERS:
WHITE TULIPS, WHITE ROSES, AND WHITE
HYDRANGEAS IN CHINOISERIE VASES

TABLETOP ELEMENTS:
WHITE ROSE PETALS STREWN ATOP WHITE
TABLES; SEAWATER BLUE SATIN NAPKINS
AND WATER GOBLETS; HURRICANE VOTIVES
FILLED WITH WATER, WHITE ROSE PETALS,
AND FLOATING CANDLES; A SINGLE
WHITE ROSE AT EACH PLACE SETTING

FOOD & DRINK:
FRENCH-MEDITERRANEAN

I set a Francophile mood the moment guests entered the courtyard with walls of hedges strung with twinkly lights and hung with classic pictures of Saint-Tropez flanking my front door. I booked the French-Mediterranean–themed restaurant Bagatelle, one of my favorites. This was the first time they'd ever entertained at an off-site event, so the uniqueness of Bagatelle at home added to the magic. It was so fabulous to have our friends experience all the fun Bagatelle has to offer—including spinning DJs, Champagne showers, and sparkler-wielding waiters who encourage guests to dance the night away on the dance floor—in a private home.

To ensure guests felt welcomed that evening, my husband, Steve, and I stood near the entrance greeting guests as waitstaff proffered Champagne, rosé, and glasses of sparkling water with slices of lime. Many people have social nerves, and the more you can do to receive them warmly, the better they will feel—and the more fun they'll have. We put our kids on host duty and had them greet guests as they entered the cocktail area, since we were stationed by the front door. A hostess handed out table cards so everyone knew where they would be seated. The more information guests have about the night to come, the more comfortable they will feel, especially at a large-scale event.

For décor, we began by filling our entryway with a festive bunch of balloons hung from the

We installed garden tents so that all could dine and dance the night away without fretting about twilight rain showers. OPPOSITE: Modern Lucite chairs, white rose petals, hurricane votives filled with water, and blue glasses add an airy appearance as effervescent as the free-flowing Champagne.

Chinoiserie vessels evoke a timeless beauty
that's perfectly suited to a milestone birthday.
White roses, hydrangeas, and tulips lend a
classical look. Three similar vases grouped
together can be more impactful than one.

ceiling. The loggia was transformed into a white wraparound bar with a ring of tablecloth-topped tables that was both surprising and architectural. We topped the bar with blue and white chinoiserie vases bursting with white tulips, white roses, and white hydrangeas. Guests mixed and mingled, enjoying cocktails, hors d'oeuvre, and a ceviche bar where tuna and salmon ceviche with all the condiments was served in martini glasses with miniature dessert spoons. After a plentiful cocktail hour, it was time for the grand reveal: opening the tents!

I prefer tents for larger parties. One, they evoke a bit of Big Top excitement and childlike wonder in all of us, no matter our age. And two, they allow you the luxury of fresh air without any of the annoyances (stiff breezes, flitting insects). Plus, when done well, tents are absolutely stunning. For this party, we chose a pleated white fabric with a blue trim border and a high gloss blue and white dance floor. An adjacent cocktail tent held another bar and seating lounge, where behind the bar we had a slideshow of fifty years of photos—a fabulous conversation starter!

Our table settings were just as transportive: at the long white tables, laden with napkins and water goblets in Mediterranean seawater blue, we flurried white rose petals, floating candles, and, this being summer, ice buckets replete with

CLOCKWISE FROM TOP LEFT: Steve and I on the night of my fiftieth birthday party. A single floral hue, such as white, maximizes the effect. Place cards at the ready. Blue and white lanterns hang in our treetops for a festive look.

chilled bottles of rosé for passing. Sushi boats from Nobu filled the centers of the tables as a first course. Later, we dined on sliced cajun chicken, pommes frites, and light garden salads inspired by Le Bilboquet, my favorite restaurant in New York City. A capiz shell chandelier shimmered overhead, casting everyone in a romantic glow as we tucked into a dessert of vanilla cake with French butter chip filling and sorbet.

Between courses that night, we gave a toast welcoming our guests—something I like to do at every event to make everyone feel included. I also delighted in speeches given by Steve, our seven children, and my girlfriends. People were crying with laughter! My preference is for a great toast to be smart and funny, not too sappy. We ended the evening with an unexpected "third act," one that Bagatelle is famous for—a raucous Champagne parade where waiters costumed as characters like Marie Antoinette and Superman hop on each other's shoulders and zip around the room with bubbly flowing and sparklers sparkling. My favorite DJ, DJ Philippe Paris, flew in from St. Barths to get the dance floor buzzing into the wee hours.

227

PREVIOUS PAGES: An abundance of candles aligned center stage on a tabletop casts party guests in an enchanting glow. Place the candles in containers of varying heights to create a tabletop "skyline" for the eye to wander. Scattering rose petals like confetti and chilling a bucket of a favorite rosé on ice says "fun" at a glance. THIS PAGE, CLOCKWISE FROM TOP LEFT: Polka dots transform a French butter cake into an edible thrill. Personalized touches, such as hand-calligraphed place cards and custom napkins, make your fête thoroughly your own. My outfit for the evening echoed the palette of the party. OPPOSITE: A fresh, fragrant bloom at each guest's place communicates, We're so glad you're here!

Izzi

Stephanie's 50th Birthday

Nobu Sushi Platter

Assorted Nigiri
Tuna · Salmon · Yellowtail
Japanese Red Snapper

"If you can dream it, you can do it."
—Walt Disney

PLANNING A BIG EVENT

IF YOU HAVE SUCCESSFULLY HOSTED A DINNER PARTY FOR TEN, you can plan an event for 200 or more—a big event requires the same planning and visualizing skills brought to a different level. Whether you are celebrating a wedding, anniversary, a graduation, or a fiftieth birthday, the key is to begin planning as early as you can—at least six months in advance. This allows plenty of time for creativity and ideas to flow.

TO MINIMIZE STRESS, begin with a highly organized timeline of deadlines.

IT'S BEST TO START WITH THE BIG DETAILS (date, location), then move to the smaller ones (band, caterer, and florist).

SENDING SAVE-THE-DATES IS A MUST in our busy world. Postmark them at least four months in advance, and the invitations themselves at least eight weeks ahead.

CREATE A CHECKLIST FOR YOURSELF for the day before and the day of that highlights everything you'll need to triple-check, from ensuring the bar is well-stocked with ice to making sure the seating arrangements are exactly as you intended them.

A LITTLE TRICK: On the day of the event, I tell all my staff to be sure everything is ready an hour before it actually needs to be. This way, the tables are set well in advance and I don't need to worry.

IN THE POWDER ROOM, I like to have a silver bowl stocked with emergency toiletries that anyone might need: Band-Aids, mints, a hairbrush, feminine hygiene products, hairspray, and the like. Anticipate the needs of your guests so they can have a seamless evening along with you.

AN HOUR BEFORE THE PARTY BEGINS, *let go*. Get dressed early, have a cocktail, and know that if something goes wrong, it's okay. Have a sense of humor! Once you've put everything in place—when the background music is on, the candles are aglow, and the cocktails prepped—it's time to put the work behind you, don your proverbial hostess hat, and enjoy yourself.

Armed with a long board of sparklers and fruit-infused vodka shots and a cake custom-lined in photographs of my beloved trio of King Charles cavaliers, Bagatelle waiters instantly energize the dance floor.

RESOURCES

ACCESSORIES AND HOME DÉCOR

1ST DIBS *1stdibs.com*

AERIN *aerin.com*

ALDIK HOME *aldikhome.com*

BACCARAT *baccarat.com*

BEACHBALLS.COM *beachballs.com*

BERGDORF GOODMAN
  bergdorfgoodman.com

BLOOMINGDALE'S *bloomingdales.com*

CHRISTOFLE *christofle.com*

DUNHILL *dunhill.com*

EMILIO PUCCI *emiliopucci.com*

EMPTY VASE *emptyvase.com*

ETSY *etsy.com*

FORTUNY *fortuny.com*

FRONTGATE *frontgate.com*

GEARYS BEVERLY HILLS *gearys.com*

HERMÈS *hermes.com*

HORCHOW *horchow.com*

JOE CARIATI *joecariati.com*

LALIQUE *lalique.com*

L'OBJET *l-objet.com*

MADELINE WEINRIB *madelineweinrib.com*

NEIMAN MARCUS *neimanmarcus.com*

POTTERY BARN *potterybarn.com*

RALPH LAUREN TEXTILES
  ralphlaurenhome.com

SCULLY AND SCULLY *scullyandscully.com*

TALMARIS, PARIS
  71 avenue mozart, 75016 paris, france

TED MUEHLING *tedmuehling.com*

TOM DIXON *tomdixon.net*

WAYFAIR *wayfair.com*

WILLIAMS SONOMA *williams-sonoma.com*

WISTERIA *wisteria.com*

ZAZZLE *zazzle.com*

CANDLES

AERIN *aerin.com*

CREATIVE CANDLES *creativecandles.com*

NEST *nestfragrances.com*

RICHARD GINORI *richardginori1735.com*

TORY BURCH *toryburch.com*

CHINA, CRYSTAL, GLASSWARE, AND SILVER

AERIN *aerin.com*

AMERICAN RAG CIE *americanrag.com*

ANDREW TANNER, REPLACEMENTS
  replacements.com

BACCARAT *baccarat.com*

BERGDORF GOODMAN
  bergdorfgoodman.com

BERNARDAUD *bernardaud.com*

CB2 *cb2.com*

CHRISTOFLE *christofle.com*

CRATE & BARREL *crateandbarrel.com*

FORTUNY *fortuny.com*

GEARYS BEVERLY HILLS *gearys.com*

HEREND *herendusa.com*

HERMÈS *hermes.com*

HORCHOW *horchow.com*

KATE SPADE *katespade.com*

LALIQUE *lalique.com*

LAURA ASHLEY *lauraashleyusa.com*

L'OBJET *l-objet.com*

MARTYN LAWRENCE BULLARD
  FOR HAVILAND *haviland.fr/en*

MIKASA *mikasa.com*

MISSONI HOME *missonihome.com/en*

MOSER *moserusa.com*

ORREFORS *orrefors.com*

REPLACEMENTS *replacements.com*

RICHARD GINORI *richardginori1735.com*

SCULLY AND SCULLY *scullyandscully.com*

TALMARIS PARIS
71 avenue mozart, 75016 paris, france

WEST ELM *westelm.com*

WILLIAM YEOWARD CRYSTAL
williamyeowardcrystal.com

WILLIAMS SONOMA *williams-sonoma.com*

EVENT PLANNING

DETAILS EVENT PLANNING: LISA
GORJESTANI *detailseventplanning.com*

FABRICS

FORTUNY *fortuny.com*

PETER DUNHAM, HOLLYWOOD
AT HOME *hollywoodathome.com*

FASHION AND JEWELRY

ANNE SISTERON *annesisteron.com*

CHANEL *chanel.com*

CHLOÉ *chloe.com*

DOLCE & GABBANA *dolcegabbana.com*

EMILIO PUCCI *emiliopucci.com*

KITON *kiton.it/en*

MANOLO BLAHNIK *manoloblahnik.com*

MISH *mishnewyork.com*

OSCAR DE LA RENTA *oscardelarenta.com*

RALPH LAUREN *ralphlauren.com*

TORY BURCH *toryburch.com*

VERDURA *verdura.com*

FLOWERS

EMPTY VASE *emptyvase.com*

FLORAL ART *floralartla.com*

THE HIDDEN GARDEN
hiddengardenflowers.com

MAYESH *mayesh.com*

INVITATIONS AND PLACE CARDS

AARDVARK LETTERPRESS
aardvarkletterpress.com

CALLIGRAPHY KATRINA
calligraphykatrina.com

PAPERLESS POST *paperlesspost.com*

VERA WANG *verawang.com*

WILLOW PAPERY *willowpapery.com*

LINENS

DEBORAH RHODES *deborahrhodes.com*

DEBORAH SHARPE LINENS
deborahsharpelinens.com

ETSY *etsy.com*

HIBISCUS LINENS *hibiscuslinens.com*

JULIA B. *juliab.com*

LA LINEN *lalinen.com*

LEONTINE LINENS *leontinelinens.com*

SFERRA *sferra.com*

TALMARIS
71 avenue mozart, 75016 paris, france

RENTALS

ACCESSORY PREVIEW
accessorypreview.com

LA TAVOLA *latavolalinen.com*

TOWN AND COUNTRY
EVENT RENTALS *tacer.biz*

THEONI LIFESTYLE EVENT RENTALS
theonicollection.com

WINE, COCKTAILS, FOOD, AND CATERING

BOND *bond.wine*

HANSEN'S CAKES *hansencake.com*

NOBU *noburestaurants.com*

WALLY'S WINE AND SPIRITS
wallywine.com

WHOA NELLIE CATERING
whoanellycatering.com

ACKNOWLEDGMENTS

It truly takes a village, and I want to thank my family and friends for all their love, support, and enthusiasm.

TO MY DARLING HUSBAND, STEVE: You have believed in me since the first day you met me and more than I ever believed in myself. Thank you for always encouraging me to be my best self. Our conversations broaden my perspective and have helped me to think more deeply and clearly and ultimately produce a better book. Thank you for your patience and for listening to me talk incessantly about colors, fabrics, flowers, and tabletop. I love you up to the sky, moon, and stars.

TO MY THREE CHILDREN (ANDE, HARRISON, AND CHARLOTTE) AND FOUR STEPCHILDREN (ANNIE, MAGGIE, REID, AND IZZI): I love all of you and our large and crazy blended family. Thank you for bringing so much joie de vivre into my life and for expanding my horizons and heart. I also want to thank each of you for being open-hearted and supportive. I cherish all the memories we have shared and the traditions we have created. I hope you take my love of entertaining and creating beautiful tabletops into your own homes.

TO MY SIBLINGS: Thank you for your love, support, and enthusiasm. Each of you has contributed to who I am today. I cherish the relationships we have created as adults and it is really fun for me to be the youngest of our tribe!

TO MY MOM AND LATE DAD, WHO EXPOSED ME TO A BEAUTIFUL LIFESTYLE IN MY EARLY YEARS: I will always be grateful for my upbringing. Your constant love of entertaining at home and enjoying our family, friends, and holiday traditions instilled in me at a very young age an appreciation for entertaining that is a large part of who I am today. I love you both dearly.

I WANT TO THANK MY FEARLESS LEADER, JILL COHEN, for putting together such a dedicated and passionate team for this book. Jill (also known as "Mama Hen," by me), you've been there for me every step of the process; thank you. It has meant the world to me that you believed in me from the start and pushed me to do my best work. You're the best in the business and you're true to your word.

TO SASHA BENEDETTO: Thank you for being there for this journey. I truly couldn't have done it without you. Your dedication, passion, and beautiful taste are admirable and have added so much to this book. You are the most resourceful person I know and you are so patient with me and my endless attention to details. Thank you for your loyalty; I am grateful.

TO THE TEAM: I am incredibly grateful for all the days and hours you dedicated to creating this beautiful book. To Andy and Gemma Ingalls: Your photography is magic and you bring to life all that we create. You are patient beyond words and team players; thank you. To Charles Miers: My first meeting at the beginning of this journey was with you. Thank you for taking on a novice and bringing Jill into my life. To Doug Turshen: Thank you for designing the most beautiful layouts. To Stephen Pappas: You are a stylist extraordinaire! You understood my taste and vision from the start and you helped execute all my expansive and colorful ideas; thank you. We both share a love of classicism and timeless beauty. You can read my mind and are a pro. To Jeanne Kelley, you are an exceptional food stylist: Your creativity and artistic talent with food is unparalleled. You are always calm, cool, and collected in the midst of chaos in the kitchen, and I thank you for that. You produced food that was decorative and delicious. Thank you for expanding my palate. To Michael Gerbino: Thank you for your talent and creativity! You followed my motto—food is décor—and you made it delicious. To Kathryn O'Shea-Evans: You have a magical way with words and you bring the pages of a book to life, so thank you. Your writing is so visual that you made me feel like I was able to enjoy every party over and over, and you transport the readers so they get to be a part of each chapter. Thank you for being so open to my direction and working with me to find my voice. To Kathleen Jayes: It has been such an honor and pleasure to work with you and Rizzoli. Your edits and direction are clear and you helped me to create a better book and experience for the reader. Thank you!

TO JEFFREY BILHUBER: A sincere thank you for spending the last seven years creating beautiful homes for Steve and me. You make a house a home and a place of serenity, beauty and joy for enjoying family and friends. Your creativity with color and your brilliance with furniture plans has inspired the way I live and entertain. Home is where the heart is—thank you for expanding my heart!

TO MY FRIENDS: My life wouldn't be the same without our friendships. Thank you for your constant encouragement and energy. You all show up and make me look good! The joy you bring me gives me reason to entertain and create these magical moments for us to share; thank you.

TO ALI SPEER: Your encouragement during our Sun Valley hikes started me on this journey—thank you! You told me, "If you can believe in it, you do it." You are a dear friend, and your positive spirit is infectious—you encourage all of us to live fully, and I adore you!

TO BLAINE LOURD: Thank you for helping make this book happen. You believed in me when I doubted myself and you never let me waiver from my end goal. Thank you for your time, wisdom, friendship, and loyalty. As you famously say, "Go, girl!!"

First published in the United States of America in 2020 by
Rizzoli International Publications, Inc.
300 Park Avenue South
New York, NY 10010
www.rizzoliusa.com

Foreword: Jeffrey Bilhuber
Text: Kathryn O'Shea-Evans
All photography by The Ingalls except:
Page 22 Christina Edwards
Pages 28, 235 Hillary Maybery

Publisher: Charles Miers
Senior Editor: Kathleen Jayes
Design: Doug Turshen with Steve Turner
Production Manager: Alyn Evans
Managing Editor: Lynn Scrabis

Developed in collaboration with Jill Cohen Associates, LLC.

Printed in Italy

2020 2021 2022 2023 / 10 9 8 7 6 5 4 3 2

ISBN: 978-0-8478-6371-6
Library of Congress Control Number: 2019950237

Visit us online:
Facebook.com/RizzoliNewYork
Twitter: @Rizzoli_Books
Instagram.com/RizzoliBooks
Pinterest.com/RizzoliBooks
Youtube.com/user/RizzoliNY
Issuu.com/Rizzoli